Jen Silverman:

THREE PLAYS

THE MOORS
THE ROOMMATE
COLLECTIVE RAGE: A PLAY IN 5 BETTIES

OBERON BOOKS
LONDON

WWW.OBERONBOOKS.COM

First published in 2018 by Oberon Books Ltd
521 Caledonian Road, London N7 9RH
Tel: +44 (0) 20 7607 3637 / Fax: +44 (0) 20 7607 3629
e-mail: info@oberonbooks.com
www.oberonbooks.com

A catalogue record for this book is available from the British
Library.

PB ISBN: 9781786824271
E ISBN: 9781786824288

Cover image by Scott Suchman

Printed and bound by 4edge Limited, Essex, UK.
eBook conversion by CPI Group (UK) Ltd, Croydon, CR0 4YY.

Visit www.oberonbooks.com to read more about all our books and to buy them. You
will also find features, author interviews and news of any author events, and you can
sign up for e-newsletters so that you're always first to hear about our new releases.

Printed on FSC accredited paper

Contents

Foreword
by Mike Donahue

Jen and I first met back in 2011, randomly assigned to work together on a ten minute play festival at New York's Ensemble Studio Theatre. I think the play had something to do with a daughter mail-ordering a naked Russian man in a box for her mother, in an attempt to get her mother to start living again. I remember haphazardly sound-designing the piece with some crass Russian pop music, and struggling to find a box that was simultaneously large enough to fit a person inside, but also—most importantly—free. (We did find one, then had to cart it all around the city on the subway for rehearsals). The festival was a quick seat-of-your-pants thing, and at the time, I'm not sure I knew I'd just found not only one of my closest collaborators, but also one of my closest friends.

After the short play festival, Jen and I stayed in touch, took road trips to see theatre by writers we both loved—and about nine months later, I got an email asking if I'd read a Jen Silverman play called *Phoebe In Winter,* because this killer downtown theatre company, Clubbed Thumb, was going to do the premiere of it. I read the play immediately, and my mind was blown. It looked nothing like what I was seeing in New York—it felt much closer to the theatre I'd so admired in Berlin while living there. It was a wild play about an avenging angel from a war-torn country inserting herself into a patriarchal family whose three sons had fought against her own brothers. She upends and militarises the family, recasting the patriarch, his sons, and their maid in one another's roles, beginning an avalanche of misalliances until the entire class and power structure has been collectively obliterated. We learned a lot together on that first production, about calibrating tone, how to invite the audience into the humour of the play while grounding its seeming absurdity in real pain, anger and history.

Since *Phoebe,* we've premiered a handful of plays together, and developed and produced a number of others. Each time we start work on a new play together, I'm challenged to articulate the tone and vocabulary of Jen's work anew. For me, Jen is a writer of limitless imagination, who constantly pushes herself to explore new approaches to structure, the rules of theatricality, and the use of language. She does this with both great rigor and unprecious playfulness. But as much as the plays may look and feel wildly different from one another, for me, Jen always writes with a sharp lens on class, gender and sexuality—and grapples with stories of transformation and power: the potential for people to change in startling and empowering ways, and the ways in which people harness and subvert status.

We premiered *The Roommate* as part of the Humana Festival of New Plays at Actors Theatre Louisville in 2015, and were able to come back to the play together in 2017, opening the main stage season of the Williamstown Theatre Festival with S. Epatha Merkerson and Jane Kaczmarek. In *The Roommate*, two women from completely different worlds crash into one another's lives. Sharon has lived a narrow fairly conformist life, and in the wake of her divorce, has resigned herself to an equally unobtrusive loneliness—but she's a misfit at heart, someone who's never actually felt at home in Midwestern domesticity. Robyn is a loner, someone whose walls are high and whose secrets are large—but at heart, she longs to leave the past behind, settle down, start over. The two women discover surprising resonances as Sharon begins to thaw Robyn's aloofness with her own disarming openness. The play unfolds in the quiet kitchen of an Iowan farmhouse, and though it initially masquerades as an odd-couple buddy comedy, even its earliest scenes are taut with deeply buried loneliness, rage, and the potential for thrilling and destructive reinventions. As Sharon and Robyn inspire one another to imagine themselves in profoundly different ways, so do they also empower each other to break and re-make the rules that have governed their lives.

In *Collective Rage: A Play In 5 Betties,* which we premiered at Woolly Mammoth Theatre Company in 2016, we meet five women, all aggressively inscribed within and unknowingly playing into particular boxes, or roles: a wealthy white Upper East Side Betty whose husband is having an affair, a bi Latinx

Betty who works at Sephora, a genderqueer Betty who's just out of prison and runs a boxing gym. The five Betties come together over a series of dinner parties, boxing lessons, and rehearsals for a devised version of the play-within-a-play from Midsummer. Through their interactions with Betties who at first glance are nothing like them, each starts to wake up to the roles in which society has cast her, and each begins to find her agency in redefining, subverting, upending, or entirely annihilating that role. Jen begins the play with an aggressive first-hit of the stereotype each woman embodies—we see them, at first glance, as they see each other. But after each deliberately crude splash of stereotype, the play surprises again and again by the ways in which each character deepens, twists and turns, expands. Betty is—all the Betties are—capable of more than we assumed about her—or what she assumed about herself. Stereotype gives way to anarchic joy.

Much like *The Roommate*, *Collective Rage* is filled with a sense of experimentation, as if completely different people were eye-droppered onto a Petri dish, in order to see what kind of chemical reactions would occur. But here, the world is stripped of naturalistic trappings—here, as soon as characters can articulate something, if they can dream something, it simply boldly becomes. Fueled by the joy of discovery, and aided by the transformational power of the theatre, the Betties rearticulate whom they can love and be attracted to, the limits they place on their intelligence and passions, and their relationship to their own bodies, strengths, and sense of self.

In *The Moors*, which was produced off-Broadway with The Playwrights Realm in 2017, Jen anachronistically invokes the world of the Brontës, albeit with a philosophically-inclined mastiff who doesn't hesitate to let us know how depressed he's become. The Moors, on which the play is set, are enigmatic and terrifyingly dangerous, an unforgiving and deliciously cruel force that can devour you whole. And yet there lurks a thrilling potential for escape from the bleak world of decorum inside the house, pervaded by loneliness and lack. Agatha, the eldest of two spinster sisters living in the old family home, was born into a patriarchal world in which she cannot rightfully wield power, in which there is no clear outlet for her undeniable intelligence—and so she has no choice but to bend and outmanoeuvre the rules of the world in order to gain control and influence. She does so with stunning logic and frank cruelty. And in spite of her best efforts, she is surprised by the discovery of a potential equal—a partner that may even, just slightly, reveal a bit of her own heart and vulnerability. The mastiff, too, discovers a potential partner: a moor-hen with a broken leg who has fallen from the sky and whose presence catalyses in him a sudden electric awakening. While the animals are unencumbered by the manipulations and tactics of the human world, they are no less endangered by the vulnerabilities of heartache. Much like Robyn in *The Roommate*, or Betty 5 in *Rage*, vulnerability is dangerous—you let your guard down, your attachments to others make you susceptible. And yet loneliness, isolation and the chance to change make the risk worth taking.

Jen and I collaborated with scenic designer Dane Laffrey on all three of these plays, which greatly influenced the way we've come to approach Jen's language in production. One of our major collaborative discoveries was the degree to which the physical space must activate and embolden her language, without burdening it. When approaching a seemingly naturalistic play like *The Roommate*, the kitchen in which it's set requires a stripped-down minimalism. We must simultaneously give the audience enough visual information to feel like Sharon actually inhabits that space, yet keep the image pared-down enough that the set doesn't clutter our ability to hear the language We found that this approach allowed the audience to stay connected to the continual micro-shifts in Sharon and Robyn's language, the very gears of how they transform one another from the moment they enter the room.

With *Collective Rage*, where the very ability to articulate something allows it to become, we found that spatial restraint was necessary. Rather than moving us between homes, gyms and rehearsal halls, or bogging us down with furniture, Dane Laffrey created a purposefully oppressive container for the space, without even perceivable entrances or exits. This both empowered the Betties to tell us where (and what) they were from moment to moment, and also facilitated a tension against which the Betties could continually push—that no matter how self-aware they become, the world they're up against continues to push back. In this way we set up the moment in which Betty 2's self-discovery literally breaks the world open—in our premiere, the final scene was ushered in by a ton of inflatable furniture, blow-up toys and balloons falling down from the grid and bouncing helter-skelter around the stage. Our brave new world was a chaotic visually playful landscape.

With *The Moors*, rather than fully realising either a period house or the moors itself, our production allowed the ever-shifting rules within the house to catalyse changes on the moors as well. The sharp edges of interior furniture were eventually consumed by the drifting fog of the exterior, and by the final scene the space was as much the one as the other. Much as Sharon learns to articulate her own deliciously destructive and liberating new future, or the Betties summon and give voice to their new identities, the inhabitants of *The Moors* similarly wield language to affect transformation.

Enjoy reading these wonderful plays, and may you find them as surprising, delightful, challenging and fulfilling as I have.

Cheers,
Mike

THE MOORS

Special thanks to my parents, who raised me on serious literature and a twisted sense of humour.

And thanks to John Baker, who offered me the Williamstown residency during which I wrote this first draft, and to Christine Scarfuto, who taught me how to breathe in the shape of a square.

THE MOORS premiered at Yale Repertory Theatre in February 2016. It was directed by Jackson Gay, set design by Alexander Woodward, costume design by Fabian Fidel Aguilar, lighting design by Andrew F. Griffin, sound design and song compostion by Daniel Kluger, and fight choreography by Rick Sordelet. The cast was as follows:

AGATHA	Kelly McAndrew
HULDEY	Birgit Huppuch
EMILIE	Miriam Silverman
MARJORY/MALLORY	Hannah Cabell
THE MASTIFF	Jeff Biehl
THE MOORHEN	Jessica Love

THE MOORS received its New York premiere with The Playwrights Realm in February 2017. It was directed by Mike Donahue, set design by Dane Laffrey, costume design by Anita Yavich, lighting design by Jen Schriever, sound design by M.L. Dogg, song composition by Daniel Kluger, and fight choreography by J. Allen Suddeth. The cast was as follows:

AGATHA	Linda Powell
HULDEY	Birgit Huppuch
EMILIE	Chasten Harmon
MARJORY/ MALLORY	Hannah Cabell
THE MASTIFF	Andrew Garman
THE MOORHEN	Teresa Avia Lim

CAST

AGATHA	F	Elder spinster sister. A steely charm. Dangerous. Powerful.
HULDEY	F	Younger spinster sister. She has a diary. Hunger propels her. She wants to be famous.
EMILIE	F	The governess. A romantic with a sweet face— but undiscovered strength at her core.
MARJORY	F	The scullery maid. Down-trodden. Vicious and strategic.
THE MASTIFF	M	The dog. A sad philosopher-king.
A MOOR-HEN	F	A small chicken. Very pragmatic.

TIME

The 1840s...ish

PLACE

The bleak moors...of England?

Think *Wuthering Heights* and *Jane Eyre* and the Brontë sisters. However: the characters all have contemporary accents native to the country of production (American, Australian, etc.) No 'period piece' accents - this play is about the present.

On casting: Casting is best when very diverse. The sisters do not have to be played by actors of the same ethnicity. There is no version in which only the animals are played by actors of color.

[ ] is unspoken, although the character is thinking it.

( ) is spoken out loud but is a side-thought.

1.

THUD!

The sound of a horrible impact that shakes our world—a bird body hitting glass.

Lights up on: the parlour of an elegant, ancient mansion on the English moors. 1840s-ish, to a degree.

AGATHA looms over HULDEY. She pulls at HULDEY's clothes, adjusts her hair. HULDEY stands like a doll and lets herself be manipulated.

The maid, MARJORY, stands to the side, waiting to be useful. MARJORY is wearing a parlourmaid hat, but when she is the scullery maid, she will put on a different hat. There is only one maid in this household.

The dog, a giant mastiff, stares despondently out of the window and thinks about how meaningless everything always seems to be.

AGATHA

Something has to be done.

MARJORY

Yes ma'am.

AGATHA

Every time one sits in the parlour, one must endure a bird crashing into the window.

MARJORY

It's terrible, ma'am.

AGATHA

See that you do something about it.

MARJORY

What would you like me to do?

AGATHA

Fix it, of course. Why am I the only one around here who takes it upon myself to fix things?

Tugging HULDEY's hair.

Do you think this is acceptable?

HULDEY

… No?

AGATHA

No, sister, it is not.
Do you know why your hair is not acceptable?

HULDEY

… No?

AGATHA

It looks like the location a particularly mangy bird might
choose to nest. Is this the sort of hair one wishes to have on
the day the governess arrives?

HULDEY
(She knows the answer to this one!)

No!

AGATHA

No, it is not that sort of hair.
What on earth have you been doing all morning?

HULDEY
(A flash of hope, she definitely knows the answer.)

Oh! Well—

AGATHA

Don't answer that.

HULDEY subsides. To MARJORY:

Is the extra room made up for the governess?

MARJORY

Yes ma'am.

AGATHA

And is there moor-hen for tonight?

MARJORY
(Isn't sure.)

Well…uh…

AGATHA

Why don't you ask the scullery maid.

MARJORY

Yes ma'am.

She is gone. The MASTIFF *raises his head. He looks at* AGATHA.

AGATHA
(Steely.)

Down.

The MASTIFF *lowers his head again.*

HULDEY

Agatha…?

AGATHA

What is it.

HULDEY

Why is there a governess coming?

A strict beat.

AGATHA

Huldeygard.

HULDEY

Yes?

AGATHA

How is it possible that you haven't washed your face?

She spit polishes HULDEY's *face.*

HULDEY

Well, this morning—

AGATHA

Don't answer that.

MARJORY returns.

MARJORY

The cook is making moor-hen, and also there are potatoes, and also the scullery maid has the typhus again.

AGATHA

Ask her if she has any sisters.

MARJORY

Sisters?

AGATHA

If she dies, perhaps one of her sisters might replace her.

MARJORY

Yes ma'am.

She leaves.

HULDEY
(Faintly, but with daring.)
You see, this morning I didn't have time to wash my face.

AGATHA

You might as well be a wild animal.

HULDEY

I was writing in my diary, you see.

AGATHA

You might as well live out on the moors with the tiny smudgy weasels.

HULDEY

And I'd reached a good part.

AGATHA

A 'good part'.

HULDEY
(Fainter.)
… Of my…uh…diary?

AGATHA

If one is not writing sums and lists and possibly strategies, then I do not know what one is writing.

HULDEY
(Brightly, taking this as an invitation.)
Oh, well, I was just writing about—

AGATHA
Don't answer that.

A beat.

I've been nourishing the hope that, since father's death, you might turn your attention to more pressing matters. You are used to having everything done for you. Father spoiled you, Branwell spoiled you, but I have no intention of spoiling you, sister.

MARJORY returns.

MARJORY
Pardon me, Miss.

AGATHA
Yes, Mallery?

MARJORY
The scullery maid has five sisters, two of whom are quite homely, two of whom are feverish, one of whom is bilious, and also there is a carriage in the driveway, it has just arrived.

AGATHA
Ah.

HULDEY
(Overwhelmed with excitement.)
The governess!

AGATHA
Show her in.

MARJORY
Yes ma'am.

She leaves. HULDEY, somewhat downtrodden, is lifted by a new wave of excitement.

HULDEY

Do you think she might be very pretty? And do you think she might like to read, perhaps she might keep a diary—?

AGATHA

If she does, we shall break her of that immediately.

The MASTIFF raises his head, also excited.

Down.

Both HULDEY and the MASTIFF sit down, eyes trained on the door. A beat of steely silence.

MARJORY enters, with EMILIE in tow. EMILIE wears a travelling cloak. She is on her best behaviour and very much wants to be liked. She carries a case for a lute (or other string instrument).

MARJORY

Miss Agatha, Miss Huldey, may I present the governess.

EMILIE
(A little breathless.)
Why hello. I'm *so* pleased to make your acquaintance, you must be...? Mistress Agatha. Mistress... Huldey. Master Branwell...?

Looks around doesn't see him.

Oh! Well. A dog! Very large dog! Nice doggy.

The MASTIFF raises his head and looks at her hopefully.

I love dogs.

AGATHA
(Cold.)
It is dangerous.

EMILIE

Ah yes?

AGATHA

It is very large and very dangerous. You must never touch it.

The MASTIFF looks at AGATHA dolefully. She hisses. He puts his head back down.

EMILIE

Oh.

AGATHA

You, I presume, are Miss Vandergaard.

EMILIE

Oh! manners! Pardon. Yes. Emilie Vandergaard, governess. In your service, I'm *so* pleased. What a long journey it's been, you must forgive me, I'm slightly scattered.

She laughs, airy and delightful.
AGATHA sizes her up.

HULDEY
(Re: the instrument case.)

… What's that?

EMILIE

This? Why, it's a lute.

HULDEY

Do you play music?

EMILIE

For the children, yes, I play lullabies sometimes.

HULDEY
(Overawed.)

Nobody ever sang to me.

AGATHA
(Breaking in, cool.)

How was your trip, Miss Vandergaard?

EMILIE

Oh, it was fine, no problems at all, a little long maybe but—

AGATHA

I'm delighted. We've been waiting for you.

EMILIE

I'm absolutely enchanted to be here.

HULDEY

Did you come from London?

EMILIE

Well, I passed through it.

HULDEY

How was it?

EMILIE

It was very big.

HULDEY
(Soft, to EMILIE.)

I'd like to see London.

AGATHA

Miss Vandergaard has only just arrived, and I'm sure she has no time to discuss... *London.*

To EMILIE.

Sit.

HULDEY subsides. EMILIE sits.
EMILIE gives the MASTIFF a tentative smile. It stares at her, mournful, without moving.

AGATHA

It will devour your face.

EMILIE

Oh!
That's dreadful!
Has it always been so savage?

AGATHA
(Decisively.)

Yes, always.
Things around here are savage things.

The moors are a savage place, and we who live here, despite our attempts to cling to a modicum of civilization, we find ourselves often forced to contend with savagery. Are you sure you're up for the task, Miss Vandergaard?

EMILIE

Oh, call me Emilie.

AGATHA

Miss Vandergaard?

EMILIE

I—well—I've been a governess many times before, if that's what you mean—I did send Master Branwell several references in my letter?

She glances around again.

Master Branwell must be out at the moment, I imagine?

AGATHA

He must be.

EMILIE

And children have always—well, I do like to think they have felt tender affections toward me—but most importantly, Miss Agatha, discipline has never been an issue.

AGATHA just stares at her. Sizing her up.

Perhaps if Master Branwell is out on a walk I might—or if he's with the horses I might just—an introduction, or a friendly hello, or—

AGATHA

I'm afraid that's not possible.

EMILIE

Not...? Oh. Of course.

Pause.

Master Branwell was kind in his letters, he spoke very highly of his sisters.

AGATHA
(Decisively.)

Miss Vandergaard.

EMILIE

Yes?

AGATHA

Dinner is always served promptly at six. One hopes not to be late for dinner.

EMILIE

Will Master Branwell be at dinner?

HULDEY looks at AGATHA. AGATHA does not even respond to the glance.

AGATHA

Master Branwell has been unwell.

EMILIE

Oh I'm so sorry. That's terrible.

AGATHA

Master Branwell may not be at dinner.

EMILIE

And the child?

HULDEY looks at AGATHA again.

AGATHA

The child. Eats in the nursery. With a maid.

EMILIE

I'm so looking forward to meeting him.

AGATHA

It is also dangerous.

EMILIE

Pardon me?

AGATHA

It is undisciplined, I said. Children of the moors are undisciplined children.

The maid will show you to your room.

MARJORY coughs. It's a wet horrible cough.
She stares at EMILIE as she coughs.

EMILIE

Oh!

HULDEY
(Brightly, confiding.)
Marjory is the scullery maid. She has the typhus, you know.

EMILIE

Oh no!

HULDEY

And the parlourmaid is Mallery. She's with child.

EMILIE

Oh my!

AGATHA

That will be all. Thank you.

EMILIE
(Stands, curtseys.)
I'm so pleased. Really quite. Grateful to be in the employ of such. Old and well-bred. Ancestral home.

AGATHA

Yes yes. Until dinner.

MARJORY

This way.

She leads EMILIE out. A moment.

HULDEY
(Wistful.)
This will all be such fun.

AGATHA

It will be many things, sister.

> *AGATHA leaves the room and HULDEY follows.*
> *A moment. And then the MASTIFF raises his head. He stares*
> *out the window at the moors.*

MASTIFF

A bird drops from the sky
like a stone in the stomach
like all your happiness
fleeting, then gone.
The gorse extends
the sky extends
many things extend.
Happiness, I suppose, does not extend.
I was once upon a time, greatly satisfied.
I believe. I do not remember clearly.
I put my face against my mother's side.
There was milk.
I imagine this caused me satisfaction.
I would not presume to call it...'happiness'.

> *Beat—sadly.*

There is nothing lasting in this world.
Birds drop and drop
there are always more
the sky keeps spitting out birds
and the birds keep dropping.
In that sense, you might say: birds are lasting, in this world.
To which I would reply: it is never the same bird.

2.

EMILIE's bedroom that seems to be the exact same room as the parlour. MARJORY leads EMILIE in. She coughs from time to time. It's a deeply jarring machine gun noise.

MARJORY

And this will be your bedroom.

EMILIE

Oh...uh...

MARJORY

Is there a problem?

EMILIE

... Is this not the parlour?

MARJORY

It's your bedroom. Ma'am.

EMILIE

... Oh, but, you see, it looks like...?

She trails away under MARJORY's baleful eye.

I see. Yes. Of course.

A beat.

MARJORY

Mistress Agatha asked to see you were settled. You look settled.

She puts on her scullery maid cap.

Now there's dishes to attend to in the scullery.

EMILIE

Just a moment.

MARJORY

Yes ma'am?

EMILIE

Which maid did you say you were?

MARJORY
(Takes off the cap.)
I'm the maid. Your maid.

EMILIE
And you have the typhus?

MARJORY
Sort of everybody's maid.
Yes, yes I do.

EMILIE
Are you the one with the typhus, or the one with the baby?

MARJORY
I'm both, sort of both.

EMILIE
How are you both of something? Either you are something, or you are another thing.

MARJORY
When I'm in the scullery, I have the typhus.
When I'm in the parlour, I have the baby.

EMILIE
Oh.

MARJORY
It's how the time passes here.

EMILIE
I see. That is one way of doing things.

MARJORY
Indeed it is.

EMILIE
I'm terribly sorry to hear about your…conditions.

MARJORY
I don't need you to be.

She turns to go again.

EMILIE

Ah—just a moment?

MARJORY

Yes ma'am.

EMILIE

How long have you worked for this household?

MARJORY

Oh. Forever, ma'am.

EMILIE

How old are you?

MARJORY

I haven't been counting. Ma'am.

EMILIE

But you were raised out here on these savage moors, you were treated kindly, perhaps they took you to church on Sundays to hear their father's sermons...? Master Branwell said—

MARJORY
(Alarmed.)

You spoke to him!

EMILIE

In the letter. He wrote me a letter.

MARJORY
(Relieved, subsiding.)

Oh.

EMILIE

... What surprises you?

MARJORY

Nothing. I'm not surprised.

EMILIE

You seem so. You seem greatly surprised.

MARJORY

No, not I.

Stand-off.

EMILIE

Is Master Branwell very frightening? Are you frightened of him?

MARJORY puts the scullery maid cap back on.

MARJORY

You'd have to ask the parlourmaid about that.

She leaves.

A moment. EMILIE looks around the parlour/bedroom. She takes a letter out of her bosom pocket. She looks at it—inquiring, troubled.

Footsteps, and HULDEY slips in.

HULDEY
(Girlish, mischievous.)

There you are!

EMILIE
(Tucks the letter away.)

Mistress Huldey!

HULDEY

Forgive me for barging into your bedroom, I know you might want some time to refresh, but I couldn't help myself. I'm so excited you're here!

EMILIE

Oh—well—thank you…

HULDEY

I just know you'll love it here! The bracing air, and the strange thorny flowers, and the gorse… And there are lots of long walks you might take. Although there's quicksand of course, and also large ravenous birds, and if you walked too far you might get turned around and lost and starve to death, or you might even be eaten by something. But in general, the moors are very pretty.

A beat.

EMILIE

Mistress Huldey—

HULDEY

Oh, just Huldey, please.

EMILIE

Huldey—

HULDEY

It sounds so wonderful how you say my name.

EMILIE

Can I ask you something?

HULDEY

Anything!

EMILIE

… Is this my bedroom?

HULDEY
(Looks around, bewildered.)

Of course.

EMILIE

Ah.
But.
Does it not—I mean—does it not look *very much* like
the parlour?

HULDEY
(Blank.)w

Does it?

A beat—charging onward.

—And father's parsonage is down the hill, and you shall like
that. Agatha and I do still enjoy going there for the sermons,
even though father's replacement is rather less exciting than
father was. But! It will be such fun to go together, to sit side
by side, we might share a hymnal, we might share gloves, we
might share shoes! I have a diary.

EMILIE
… I'm sorry?

HULDEY
(Staring at her very intently now.)
A diary. I keep one.

EMILIE
Well that's lovely.

HULDEY
It is very exceedingly personal and private of course, I shouldn't like to tell you what I write in it. I have a very active imagination.

EMILIE
Master Branwell—is he also a man of God?

HULDEY
No, I wouldn't say that.

EMILIE
A kind man, would you say? A gentle one?

HULDEY
Do you keep a diary, Emilie? (May I call you Emilie?)

EMILIE
I don't keep a diary, I'm afraid.

HULDEY
Oh that's too bad. That's too bad. But you might start!

EMILIE
I…might, I suppose.

HULDEY
(Delighted.)
You might start tonight, if you wanted.

EMILIE
I'm not much of a writer, I have to confess—

HULDEY
It's not hard at all, I could help you. What you do is, you begin with a heading: MONDAY, for example, and then you just write

down what you feel. And when you have a different feeling, you write down a different header, TUESDAY, for example—

EMILIE
(Laughing.)
But you can't just start a new day whenever you like.

HULDEY
Of course you can. That's how the time works out here.

EMILIE
… Well, that's very helpful, I'll consider it.
If you don't mind my asking about your brother—

HULDEY
You might write about London, too. You might describe what it was like.

EMILIE
I—yes, I suppose I could.

HULDEY
And then you might read it to me. For example, I've heard that in London, one gets murdered.

EMILIE
Murdered?

HULDEY
Most horribly murdered, I've heard.

A beat. EMILIE tries again.

EMILIE
Would you describe your brother as a gentle man, do you think, Huldey?

HULDEY
My brother?

EMILIE
Yes.

HULDEY
Describe him?

EMILIE

For example—he had a very nice hand. In his letters.

HULDEY

Did he.

EMILIE

A very *gentle* and well-formed hand.

HULDEY

That's nice.

EMILIE

And the words he used were educated ones.

HULDEY

Yes, well.
There's lots of time out here. In which to be educated in one thing or another.

EMILIE

But I imagine your brother went to study somewhere?
London, perhaps? France?

HULDEY

Ah. Well. Studying.
Master Branwell. Was not. Studying, was not.
Quite.

EMILIE

Just like a boy. I imagine he preferred lively debates about the law, and dances, perhaps?

HULDEY

Hmm.

EMILIE

I'm so looking forward to meeting your brother—and the child—

HULDEY
(A little desperate.)

It will be so lovely to have another person here, one that one might talk to, might sit by the fire on a lonely night and just —

JEN SILVERMAN

I might read you a page or two from my diary, if you very much wished it.

EMILIE
(Alarmed.)
That wouldn't be necessary, I'm sure.

HULDEY
It's very vivid and upsetting, and I might, I might, if you *very much*—

EMILIE
Oh, no—

HULDEY
Just one page, or two, or perhaps a chapter, or—

EMILIE
We should both get ready for dinner, don't you think?

HULDEY
(Deeply disappointed.)
Oh.
Well.
Indeed.
I should.
Before dinner.

She leaves.

EMILIE, alone, even more bewildered.

3.

The MASTIFF. Out on the moors.
He stares up at the sky.
The sky is bleak.
The light is very sharp and clear.
All of it extends forever.
Birds fly, high up and far away.
The MASTIFF is utterly alone.

MASTIFF

The pursuit of the ephemeral.
There is joy in it. To be sure.
Your fingers close around the thing,
it eludes you,
you desire more,
more eludes you,
frustration and ecstasy are nearly the same sensation.
Whole religions are based on this.
Also, it appears, relationships.

The MASTIFF closes his eyes.

'God.'
'Hello God.'
This is called prayer.
I talk, and you are silent.
Whole relationships are based on this as well.

A bird drops from the sky.
It is a MOOR-HEN.
It crash-lands.

MOOR-HEN

Ahhhhh!

MASTIFF

You!

MOOR-HEN

I hate this!

MASTIFF

God!

MOOR-HEN

Flying! It's the worst!
... Sorry?

MASTIFF

It's you!

MOOR-HEN

Do we know each other?

MASTIFF
(Double takes.)

You look like a moor-hen.

MOOR-HEN

I am a moor-hen.

MASTIFF

Are you God, and *also* a moor-hen?

MOOR-HEN

This is a very circuitous line of questioning.

MASTIFF

I'm confused.

MOOR-HEN

I am a moor-hen. I hate flying. It makes me queasy. I hate
landing. Well. No. I hate the takeoff and I also hate the
landing, but the actual part where I'm in the air, albeit brief,
is not as hateful to me. In general. What were you asking me?

MASTIFF

Are you God or are you a moor-hen?

MOOR-HEN

What is... 'God'.

MASTIFF

Or did God send you?

MOOR-HEN

Nobody sends me. I make my own decisions.

Beat. They take each other in. Cautiously.

This... 'God'. It lives in the sky?

MASTIFF

Did you see Him on your way down?

MOOR-HEN

Is it a very large bird?

MASTIFF

I don't think so.

MOOR-HEN

But you saw it fly over?

MASTIFF

No, He lives there. The father of my house knew Him intimately.

MOOR-HEN
(Baffled.)

Were you going to eat 'God'?

MASTIFF

No! No. I just wanted to talk.

MOOR-HEN

I don't understand you at all.

She turns to go.

MASTIFF

Wait!

MOOR-HEN

What is it.

MASTIFF

What do you think of happiness?

MOOR-HEN

Of what-now?

                    MASTIFF

Happiness?

                    MOOR-HEN

I don't know what that is.

                    MASTIFF

It's this feeling like a clench, like a fist, like right where your
heart is but further underneath. It hurts and then it's gone,
and then you want it again.

                    MOOR-HEN

So…indigestion.

                    MASTIFF

I don't think…

                    MOOR-HEN

Or hunger.

                    MASTIFF

Not exactly…

                    MOOR-HEN

Like in the winters when there aren't enough berries or seeds
or anything really and the clench-knot-fist in your stomach
area hurts. And then spring comes! And there are berries and
seeds. And bugs. Fat grubby grubs. And it goes away.

                    MASTIFF

No.

                    MOOR-HEN

Oh.
Then…no.

     Turns to go.

                    MASTIFF

Wait!

                    MOOR-HEN

Wait what!

MASTIFF

I just want to talk to you.

MOOR-HEN

You're very large. You look very large. You look like perhaps
something that might eat me.

MASTIFF

I don't intend to.

MOOR-HEN

But you admit that you are very large?

MASTIFF

I guess so.

MOOR-HEN

Well, there you go.

The MOOR-HEN turns to go.

MASTIFF

I'm very lonely.

MOOR-HEN

You're…what-now?

MASTIFF

Lonely. It's that thing—that clench—that fist in your stomach
except this time it *doesn't* go away, and you *don't* want it.

MOOR-HEN

You're hungry. And I'm small. And I think I should go now.

The MOOR-HEN leaves.

The MASTIFF sits alone.

MASTIFF

Well.
That didn't go very well.
The moors swallow all the sound.
We don't even hear our own intentions, after a time.
We're just filled with the sound
of things getting lost.

4.

After dinner, in the Second Sitting Room...which appears to be the same room as the parlour. AGATHA crochets. HULDEY and EMILIE sip tea. MARJORY serves the tea. She wears a parlourmaid hat. THE MASTIFF lies by the window.

HULDEY

Dinner is very spare. Most things here, you'll find, are spare.

EMILIE

Oh no, not at all.

HULDEY

I'm sure it's not what you're used to.

EMILIE

I don't mind in the slightest.

HULDEY

But it is rather nice to sit in the Second Sitting Room after dinner, we so rarely use it. Isn't it nice?

EMILIE
(Sotto.)
... Are we not in the parlour?

HULDEY
(Confused.)
No, this is the Second Sitting Room.

EMILIE

... Oh.

HULDEY

You've been all over, haven't you. How wonderful to have seen all the things you've seen!

EMILIE

I've been employed in many houses, but what one sees does not change so very much, I've found.

HULDEY

I've never seen anything.

AGATHA

Mallory.

MARJORY

Yes ma'am.

AGATHA

Are you using the good teacups?

MARJORY

Yes ma'am.

AGATHA

And why is that.

MARJORY

Company, ma'am.

AGATHA

Miss Vandergaard is not company, Mallory. She's come to stay with us. She will be part of the family, now.

MARJORY

Yes ma'am.

AGATHA

That will be all.

MARJORY curtseys and leaves.

EMILIE

… Was that not Marjory?

AGATHA

Marjory is the scullery maid.
Mallory is the parlourmaid.

EMILIE

Yes…
But in actuality, was that not…?

MARJORY re-enters. Scullery maid hat.

AGATHA

What is it, Marjory.

MARJORY

I'm sent to inform you, the rest of the teacups have been broke, Ma'am.

AGATHA

Broke?

MARJORY

Master Branwell...

AGATHA

Ah. Yes. I see.

MARJORY

That one time...

AGATHA

Yes yes. Nevermind. That will be all.

MARJORY

Yes ma'am.

She exits. A beat.

HULDEY

I'm sure there were lots of grand after-dinner diversions in the other houses? Games and parties and desserts perhaps?

EMILIE

I don't know...

HULDEY

What kinds of things did you do?

EMILIE

Nothing special... Sometimes I played a song or two, when the children asked.

HULDEY

What if you sang us a song now?

She looks at AGATHA hopefully. EMILIE tries to gauge AGATHA's expression and fails.

EMILIE

Oh, I wouldn't like to impose…

HULDEY

She might play for us, Agatha, mightn't she?

EMILIE

It's just silliness, Huldey, your sister wouldn't want to be bothered with it.

A moment. AGATHA sizes her up. Then:

AGATHA
(Cool.)

Why don't you play for us.

EMILIE

Are you sure?

AGATHA

In your letter to Master Branwell, you mentioned your particular love of music. I must imagine that you're quite good. Are you not quite good?

EMILIE
(Flustered.)

Master Branwell mentioned that to you?

AGATHA

Are you good, or are you not good.

A beat. EMILIE meets AGATHA's eyes. A little responding steeliness.

EMILIE

I'm fairly good.

AGATHA

Fairly?

EMILIE

I'm quite good.

AGATHA

I'll be the judge of that.

HULDEY glances uneasily between them.

EMILIE

I should be delighted to oblige.

She takes out her lute. She sings a song.
It's simple enough, but she's very good. It's strangely plaintive
and haunting. It fills the space in a way that few things have
filled it.

As she plays, MARJORY sneaks back in and listens. The MASTIFF
lifts his head.

The song touches each of them in a way they didn't expect.

EMILIE'S SONG

When I was a child, I felt as a child
When I was a woman, I felt something new
When I become old, I'll turn to bone or heather
When I die the winds will cry but the sky will still be blue.

When you were a child, you thought as a child
When you were a woman, you thought something new
When you become old, you'll change just like the weather
When you die the winds will cry but the sun will still shine through.

There's a haunting wind in the streets tonight
There's a silver moon so cold
I travelled far from my bed tonight
Your love makes me over-bold
There's the taste of change in the air tonight
A story never told

Oh for a life where we're simple as the stars
Oh for a life where we're freer than the grass
Oh for a life where we're bolder than the daybreak
And oh for a life where, like the time, we pass.

EMILIE finishes her song.

MARJORY withdraws, unseen.
HULDEY is moved nearly to tears. AGATHA feels something stir inside her that's shocking and new. She pushes it down.

AGATHA

Well. That was passable.

EMILIE

It was quite good.

HULDEY
(A dawning joy.)
It's so sad.

EMILIE

Would you like to sing, Miss Agatha?

AGATHA

No.

EMILIE

No?

AGATHA

Perish the thought.

HULDEY
(Real pleasure.)
You made me feel...so sad.

EMILIE

Master Branwell says that there is nothing he enjoys more than a woman of many talents. Perhaps he might like to sing with us.

AGATHA

My brother had an eye for women, talented or otherwise.

EMILIE

I'm sure he means no harm by it.

AGATHA

Oh, are you sure?

Slight beat.

HULDEY
I've never made anybody feel as sad as that.

Slight beat.

EMILIE
Miss Agatha.

AGATHA
Yes.

EMILIE
In the past few hours since my arrival, have I given you any particular reason to dislike me?

A real beat.

AGATHA
Huldey. Would you be so kind.

HULDEY
What.

AGATHA
(Indicating she should leave.)
Would you. Be. *So* kind.

> *HULDEY feels this rejection deeply.*
> *She looks to EMILIE for help.*
> *EMILIE doesn't say anything.*
> *HULDEY feels the betrayal.*

HULDEY
I had somewhere else to be anyway.

HULDEY leaves.

A moment.

AGATHA
Master Branwell is dead.

EMILIE
That is not possible.

AGATHA

Of course it is *possible*, child.
All things here are *possible*.

EMILIE

But I— From his very hand, I received—

AGATHA

Master Branwell suffered greatly from the typhus.
And then he passed.

EMILIE

But—the letter. All the letters.

AGATHA

Did you like them?

EMILIE

Did I...?

AGATHA

Did you enjoy them. Did you feel...generously toward their author.

EMILIE

They were very...affectionate letters.

AGATHA

They coaxed from you a warmth. Did they not. You responded
in kind. Your affection grew.

EMILIE

When did Master Branwell pass?

AGATHA

Three months ago, give or take.

EMILIE

But...that cannot be possible, you see, for the letters—

AGATHA

They were by my hand.

    A beat.

EMILIE

I don't believe you.

AGATHA

You think I cannot write…affectionately, when I choose?

EMILIE

That was not a woman's hand. A woman would not be capable
of such letters.

AGATHA

I think, Miss Vandergaard, you know very little about women
and what they are capable of. That is not your fault. You
have been handed limitations, which you accepted. Perhaps
accepting them *was* your fault. Either way, in your time here on
the moors, perhaps you will become more knowledgeable.

   A beat.

EMILIE

What am I doing here?

AGATHA

Pardon?

EMILIE

I came at the request of Master Branwell—yet I find he is dead.
I'm here to look after a child—that I have not met, and that
you seem in no hurry to have me meet. If I am not here for
Master Branwell, or for the child, then what precisely is it for?

AGATHA

Do you wish to leave?

EMILIE

It was a question.

AGATHA

No one is a prisoner here, Emilie. If you are eager to return
to London and seek yet another poorly paid position in yet
another syphilitic household, you have only to repack your trunk.

EMILIE

It was only a question.

AGATHA

I didn't quite hear you.

EMILIE

I am not...eager.

AGATHA

Well then. More tea?

EMILIE

Excuse me?

AGATHA

Would you enjoy more tea?
Mallory!

MARJORY enters. Parlour hat. Curtseys. Tea.

My brother was a rageful man. So. There is that.
He broke the teacups. As you have heard.
Other things, too, were broken.
Dolls. When we were younger.
Eventually a neck or two.
He had his way with the maid, on multiple occasions.

EMILIE

With Marjory??

AGATHA

With Mallory.

EMILIE

But in actuality—?

AGATHA

Master Branwell was not a prudent man.

A beat.

EMILIE

Were *any* of the letters from Branwell?

AGATHA

Perhaps the first. What did the first say?

EMILIE

It notified me that my advertisement had come to his attention, and that his household was seeking a governess.

AGATHA

Oh. Yes. No. That was still myself.

EMILIE

And the…poetry? The…descriptions?

AGATHA

(Can't help a little pride.)
You did like them, didn't you.

EMILIE

How can you sit there before me and admit to writing things of such a nature!

AGATHA

If they were badly written, that would be a different matter. None of what you received was badly written, don't you agree?

EMILIE

Badly written or not, it was shameless!

AGATHA

'Shameless'.

EMILIE

A woman ought never—

AGATHA

A *woman*, Miss Vandergaard, desires results. A little girl desires approval, maybe. But a *woman* desires efficient results. I desired a governess. I wrote to one. She quit her immediate position and she came to me. Like a bee to a flower. Is that not…efficient? Is that not what you would call: a result?

Beat.

EMILIE

And now that I am here?

AGATHA

Now that you are here, you should rest. It's been quite a journey.

EMILIE

And your intentions? And the reason—?

AGATHA

You were right.

EMILIE

… Excuse me?

AGATHA

Your song was more than passable.

A beat between them.

Mallory. Please show Miss Vandergaard to her bedroom.

MARJORY

Yes ma'am.

EMILIE

But…

AGATHA

Good night.

AGATHA stands. After a beat, EMILIE stands.
She follows MARJORY out.

The MASTIFF glances up at AGATHA.

AGATHA

Down.

AGATHA leaves the room as well.

5.

HULDEY enters, diary in hand.
She addresses the MASTIFF.

HULDEY

Ah! You!

The MASTIFF looks at her dolefully. Re: her diary:

Oh, this?
Well if you insist, but just a little bit.
My diary is extremely private you see—
but since you ask so nicely—
but I have to warn you it is *very very* sad.

She reads from her diary.

Monday: I am very unhappy.
Tuesday: It is bleak here, and I am unhappy.
Wednesday: There was fog, and my digestive system was
disagreeable, and I was greatly unhappy.
Thursday: There is a driving rain on the moors, and a
governess arrived, she has beautiful hair and I think we shall be
best friends, closer than sisters.

A new feeling, in the moment:

Friday: The governess does not seem to keep a diary.

Beat. She looks at the MASTIFF. He looks back.

It's hard to be rather well-known. I wouldn't say *famous*—but
someone else might. Whenever I go to the village, everybody
says, 'There is the parson's youngest daughter.' They say,
'I wonder what exciting thing she is thinking today!' They say,
'I hear she's a famous writer.' And one doesn't like to be talked
about all the time, it makes one feel quite uncomfortable, so I
say, 'Oh stop, I'm just like you, there's nothing special about me
at all.' And they just *refuse* to believe me. They think I'm special.
They think it's so very evident, when they look at me, that I was
destined for wonderful things, even if I can't see those things
myself, it's so very evident to every last one of them.

Beat. HULDEY bursts into tears.

THE MASTIFF takes a deep breath.
He tries to communicate to HULDEY in her preferred medium.

MASTIFF

Monday.
I met God.
He was a moor-hen, and He fled from me.
Was I supposed to pursue?

HULDEY
(Hearing none of this—crossly.)
Oh just go away. Big awful dog. Snuffling on everything.
I hate it here. I hate everything. I hate you.

She throws her diary at him.

The MASTIFF sighs and leaves.

6.

The MOOR-HEN sits, leg at a bad angle.
The MASTIFF approaches.

MASTIFF

Hello.

MOOR-HEN

Aaaaaah!

MASTIFF

It's just me.

MOOR-HEN

Have we met?

MASTIFF

Yes! You fell from the sky. You dislike flying. I asked you about God.

MOOR-HEN

Oh! Yes. You were difficult. To understand. But not disagreeable.

MASTIFF

Thank you.

MOOR-HEN

But uncomfortably large.

MASTIFF

What's wrong with your leg?

MOOR-HEN

Crash-landing.

MASTIFF

That looks painful.

MOOR-HEN

It isn't the most fun I've ever had.

MASTIFF

Do you need help?

MOOR-HEN

What help! You stay over there.

MASTIFF

Good help. Non-violent help.

MOOR-HEN

Unless you can grow me another leg, I don't see how you'd help.

MASTIFF

I could set your leg at a better angle.
I could make you soup.

MOOR-HEN

Why would you do any of those things.

MASTIFF

I want us to talk.

MOOR-HEN

Why?

MASTIFF
(Faster and faster.)
Because nobody ever talks to me, and I never talk to anybody.
And I have so many thoughts.
I stay up late at night. With all my thoughts.
They echo around inside my head.
Until it gets so everything seems terrible and sharp-edged and awful.
I can't remember that there was ever anything good at all.
And people look at my face. They look at my face and they see nothing.
They think there are no expressions on my face, just because they don't know how to look for the expressions that *are* on my face.
They think I'm guarded. But actually, if anybody truly *asked* me anything, I would tell them! I don't want to be all alone with my thoughts! It's like being in a dark room all the time and you don't have any hands and nobody thinks to open the door for you!

Deep breath.

Sorry.

I'm sorry.

I didn't mean to say all of that.

I'm just not used to anybody listening.

MOOR-HEN

How do you know I'm listening?

MASTIFF

You might not be, but you're sitting still and looking at me, and that's good enough.

Beat.

He approaches. This time, she lets him get pretty close. And then stops him.

MOOR-HEN

That's close enough.

MASTIFF

I've been thinking about you a lot.

MOOR-HEN
(A little flattered, also alarmed.)

Have you?

MASTIFF

I addressed God, and then there you were. It can't be a coincidence.

MOOR-HEN

Look, I don't know what a coincidence is, but sometimes things just happen, you know?

MASTIFF

That's called a coincidence.

MOOR-HEN

Oh!

Beat.

MASTIFF

But I've just been talking about me. I want to know about you.
If flying doesn't make you happy, why do you do it?

MOOR-HEN

Happy?

MASTIFF

We talked about this.

MOOR-HEN

I have a terrible memory. It's why I never really learn new things.
But also, I don't worry all that much, so it works for me, in a
limited way.

MASTIFF

It's this clench-knot— nevermind.
Tell me about flying.

MOOR-HEN

Well. When I'm up, I'm up and up and up!
… And then I'm DOWN.
And then usually something hurts.
And this time, something hurts a lot.

MASTIFF

Are you sure you don't want me to take a look at it?

MOOR-HEN

You just stay right where you are.

MASTIFF

I used to imagine that if I could fly, it would make me happy.
To just…from high above, look down at things.
I imagine that if you can see the parameters of things, you can
love them. I imagine that's why God loves everybody. And also
because he doesn't actually have to be touched by us.

MOOR-HEN

I've been up there. It's not that great.

MASTIFF

Oh.

Beat.

> **MOOR-HEN**

Look.

> **MASTIFF**

Yes?

> **MOOR-HEN**

You look like a squashed grub. Like a little flat grub with its insides coming out of its outsides.

> **MASTIFF**

I'm depressed.

> **MOOR-HEN**

I don't know what that is.

> **MASTIFF**

It's a little flat grub with its insides coming out of its outsides.

> **MOOR-HEN**

Shouldn't you do something about that?

> **MASTIFF**

I'm talking to you.

> **MOOR-HEN**

Oh.
And are you feeling less…'depressed'?

> **MASTIFF**

I think so, yes.

> **MOOR-HEN**
> *(Baffled, flattered.)*

Oh!

Beat. It starts to rain.

Great. Just great.
This day sucks.

> **MASTIFF**

Can I come closer?

MOOR-HEN

Why?

MASTIFF

Because I am very big and you are very small and it's raining, and if I stand over you, I will get all the rain, and none of it will reach you.

MOOR-HEN

Oh.
Well.
Hmm.

MASTIFF

And I won't eat you at all.

MOOR-HEN

Well okay but just this time.

> *The MASTIFF walks to the MOOR-HEN.*
> *He shields her from the rain.*
> *It's intimate and amazing and terrifying.*

MOOR-HEN

Are you cold?

MASTIFF

No.

MOOR-HEN

You're shaking.

MASTIFF

I've never been this close to someone.

MOOR-HEN

That can't be true.

MASTIFF

I've never been this close to someone who was actually looking at me.

MOOR-HEN

I can close my eyes.

MASTIFF

No! No.
Don't close your eyes.
Please.

MOOR-HEN

Okay then.

MASTIFF

I have the strangest...sensation.

MOOR-HEN

Is it the typhus?

MASTIFF

It's this feeling
in my heart-cavern
as if spring has come
and all the birds are falling upwards.

They stand. It rains.
The MASTIFF falls in love.

7.

MARJORY polishes shiny things in the scullery. EMILIE appears in the doorway.

EMILIE

There you are!

MARJORY is startled.

I didn't mean to startle you.

MARJORY

I'm not startled.

EMILIE

Are you Marjory or Mallory right now?

MARJORY

I'm in the scullery, so I'm the scullery maid.

EMILIE

… Is this the scullery?

MARJORY

What does it look like.

A beat. Let's not answer this.

EMILIE zeroes in on MARJORY.

EMILIE

Yes-typhus, no-baby?

MARJORY

Very good.

EMILIE

How's the baby?

MARJORY

Unwanted.

EMILIE

Which is preferable, typhus or a child?

MARJORY

Well, neither is preferable.

EMILIE

You have a point.

MARJORY

Which is preferable, being a governess in London, or being a governess here?

EMILIE

London, probably. Maybe not.

MARJORY

Which is preferable, being eaten by wolves, or being a governess?

EMILIE

Is that a joke?

MARJORY

Did you find it funny?

EMILIE

Not particularly.

MARJORY

Then it wasn't a joke.

Beat.

EMILIE

You knew that Master Branwell was dead, and you didn't say a word to me.

MARJORY

I don't know anything.

EMILIE

He's been dead three months.

MARJORY

If you say so.

EMILIE
(Alarmed.)

Is he dead or isn't he?

MARJORY

He's whatever Mistress Agatha says he is.

EMILIE

I don't like that answer at all.

MARJORY

I have to go polish things.

EMILIE

You just keep on polishing. Right here.

MARJORY

No, I have to go to a place where you aren't, and polish things.

Beat.

EMILIE

Do you like sweets? I'll give you a sweet.

MARJORY

God doesn't like sweet things.

EMILIE

Or a pretty piece of lace. I have some pretty lace I brought all the way from London.

MARJORY

God doesn't like pretty things either.

EMILIE

What do you want?

Beat.

MARJORY

You do this.

EMILIE

What?

MARJORY hands her the polishing cloth.

MARJORY

You.

Beat. EMILIE laughs. MARJORY doesn't.
Beat. EMILIE takes the cloth.

Beat.

Go on.

EMILIE

I— what do I—?

MARJORY

You scrub.

EMILIE
(Laughing.)

This is really rather...

MARJORY

God loves women. On their knees. Scrubbing.

Beat. EMILIE sees MARJORY isn't kidding.
Beat. EMILIE tentatively polishes.

Harder.

Scrubs harder.

Harder.

Scrubs harder.

Harder than that.

EMILIE scrubs harder than that.
MARJORY watches, no expression on her face.

EMILIE
(Scrubbing.)

Is Branwell dead or alive?

MARJORY

You have to put your back into it.

EMILIE
(Putting her back into it.)
And where is the child I'm to watch? I've been here two days already.

MARJORY

You're not doing it right.

EMILIE
(Frustrated.)
How am I not doing it right!

MARJORY

You'd do it better if you had the typhus, I think.

EMILIE

This is all a little much.

MARJORY

Come closer.

EMILIE

What.

> *MARJORY leans forward and coughs in EMILIE's face. EMILIE steps back, shocked.*

MARJORY

There you go.
Now scrub.

EMILIE

Now look here—!

MARJORY

Master Branwell is living in the attic. If you want to call that 'living'.
You want more? Scrub like you mean it.

> *A shocked beat. EMILIE does want more.*
> *She scrubs again.*

EMILIE

Whatever is he doing in the attic?

MARJORY

You'd scrub better if you were pregnant, I think. Come here.

EMILIE
(Completely alarmed.)

No!

MARJORY

Do you want to know what it is to scrub well, or don't you?

EMILIE

Why is he in the attic!

MARJORY

Before she laid the last brick. There was a small ray of light coming through the brick wall, where the hole was, and he put his face to it. He could barely reach, because of the chains. But he put his mouth to it as if he could drink the sunlight. He said: 'Don't do this.' But he knew she would do it, of course.

EMILIE

Who? Who would do such a thing?

MARJORY approaches her, with a cold stare.
It's utterly disconcerting.

MARJORY

Close your eyes.

EMILIE

I don't want to.

MARJORY

But I didn't ask. What you wanted.
I didn't ask that.

EMILIE
(Backed into a corner.)

I want to go home.

MARJORY

This is your home, isn't it? This is your home now.

AGATHA enters.

AGATHA

Mallory.

MARJORY
(Immediately transformed.)

Yes ma'am.

AGATHA

What *are* you doing.

MARJORY

Showing Miss Vandergaard the...scullery, ma'am.

AGATHA

She does not need to see it.

MARJORY

Yes ma'am.

AGATHA

You are a very idle girl, Marjory. Go and make yourself useful elsewhere.

MARJORY

Yes ma'am.

She exits.

A beat between AGATHA and EMILIE.

AGATHA

Did she upset you?

EMILIE
(Very upset.)

Not at all.

AGATHA

You seem as if you might cry.

EMILIE

I don't believe in crying.

AGATHA takes EMILIE in, with grudging respect. The thing she felt during the song flickers for her again.

AGATHA

... Perhaps you would like to take a walk.

EMILIE

A walk?

AGATHA

We have some matters to discuss. Where better to do so than on the moors. The fresh air. The day light. The brisk wind.

EMILIE

And the quicksand? And the ravenous birds?

AGATHA

You shall enjoy it all immensely.

And as they move, the whole world transforms...

8.

The moors. AGATHA and EMILIE.
The skies go on forever.
The light is hypnotic and terrifying and beautiful.

AGATHA

What do you think?

EMILIE

It's rather...large.

AGATHA

Yes.

EMILIE

And cold.

AGATHA

Yes.

EMILIE

One might get lost out here, so easily.

AGATHA

One wrong turn and it's all over.

EMILIE

I don't even know where the house is.

AGATHA

One might look around in all directions and see no sign of civilization whatsoever.

Beat.

EMILIE

Does it not seem very lonely to you?

AGATHA

I find it comforting.

EMILIE

Comforting?

AGATHA

I cannot stand weakness. I cannot stand it in myself, and I cannot
abide it in others.

There is no weakness in the moors.

When I come out here, I am surrounded by merciless strength.

EMILIE

But mightn't it turn on you? Mightn't you be devoured by it?

AGATHA

Yes, absolutely.

A beat. EMILIE is impressed despite herself.

EMILIE

The maid says you bricked Master Branwell in the attic.

AGATHA

Which maid was it?

EMILIE

Marjory.
Mallory.
Is it untrue?

AGATHA

No, no. All true.

EMILIE

That's horrible!

AGATHA
(A real question.)

Why is it horrible?

EMILIE thinks about this.

EMILIE

Well. He was your brother.

AGATHA

He gambled. He deflowered virgins. He ran up considerable
debts.

EMILIE

So you chose to punish him for his ungodly ways?

AGATHA

Oh. No. One gets tired of cleaning up after others. And then one wishes to be rid of them.

EMILIE

That's it?

AGATHA

After father died, Branwell's indiscretions made life particularly irritating. Life became much less irritating when Branwell was in the attic.

EMILIE

Is he dead?

AGATHA

I left him with a loaf of bread.
Of course, one loaf of bread does not last for three months.

    Beat.

EMILIE
(This isn't a bad thing.)
You are very heartless and cruel.

AGATHA

No. You see, that is a common fallacy. That strength on the part of humans is cruelty. Here upon the moors, do you think one is coddled? No. A bird or a fox or a dragonfly, it must survive from sheer strength and will alone. And does one call the moors 'cruel'? 'Heartless'? No. One accepts them for what they are. Inhospitable, perhaps. But that is their nature. One accepts that nature—and only by accepting, nay, embracing it, can one truly be at home here.

EMILIE

You are unlike anyone I have ever met.

AGATHA

And what do you make of it?

Beat. The spark between them intensifies.

EMILIE

Did you truly write those letters?

AGATHA

I did.

EMILIE

And you read my letters.

AGATHA

Of course.

EMILIE

Did you read them in the parlour? Or did you wait until you were in your bed-chamber?

AGATHA

Oh, I chose the privacy of my bed-chamber.

EMILIE
(Shy.)

And did they...delight you?

AGATHA

I found them very instructive.

EMILIE

Instructive...?

AGATHA

I found them quite telling. I read into them a great deal about your character, and its weaknesses, and how easily you find yourself at the mercy of the world.

EMILIE
(Bold.)

But pleasure, Agatha. Did you find in them any...pleasure?

AGATHA sizes her up. AGATHA smiles.

AGATHA

Have you ever had a love affair, little Emilie?

EMILIE

One doesn't talk about such things.

AGATHA

One doesn't. You're right. One does not.
But here we are, and we are entirely alone...

EMILIE

When I—when I read his letters—your letters—they made me strangely—warm.

AGATHA

Did they.

EMILIE

A sort of a...pins and needles feeling. In all my extremities. Even my toes.

AGATHA

And did you like it?

EMILIE

Oh, it was very dangerous.

AGATHA

Did *you* take these letters to bed with you? Did you sleep with them against your skin?

EMILIE

I might have.

AGATHA

And you did it so you could dream of him.

EMILIE

I—yes, maybe I did.

AGATHA

And you did, you did dream of me, and it was very nice. Wasn't it.

EMILIE

It was.

AGATHA

In your dream you came to this house. And that first night at the dinner table, he had eyes only for you.

EMILIE

He stared at me with bright, dark eyes. He saw me.

AGATHA

And you were seen, as you had never before been seen.

EMILIE

And days passed, of course. One doesn't move too quickly.

AGATHA

And then one night I came to your room, I stood in your door.

EMILIE

It was a dark night, only the hint of a moon.

AGATHA

And the roughness of my stubble against your palm.

EMILIE

Against my cheek.

AGATHA touches her cheek.

AGATHA

The roughness of my hands.

EMILIE

And everything so dark, it's hard to see—

AGATHA

—and no time to stop…

EMILIE

And I did not wish to.

AGATHA

You did not wish to stop.

AGATHA kisses EMILIE. EMILIE could live in that kiss, but eventually AGATHA breaks it.

You asked why I brought you here.

EMILIE

It doesn't matter.

AGATHA

Of course it matters.
I have brought you here to claim greatness.

EMILIE

Greatness?

AGATHA

My sister, as you have seen, is worthless.
My brother was worse.
The maid is beyond hope.
But you...you will obey me, little Emilie.

EMILIE

I...will?

AGATHA

With great precision and determination and unswerving loyalty.
You will do so because, for the first time in your short and
unremarkable life, you have been chosen. Above others,
over others. You, and only you. And your future will be unlike
any other.

EMILIE

Did you really consider others?

AGATHA

I did.

EMILIE

(This means a lot to her.)
... Oh.

AGATHA

Master Branwell is in the attic. As you know.
What you do not know is this: while he may be close to death,
he is not yet dead.
Marjory brings him a thin gruel, to keep him on this side of life.

She moves aside the final brick, as it has not yet been mortared, and she pours that thin gruel through the hole and into his weak and waiting mouth.

EMILIE
Why have you chosen to keep him alive?

AGATHA
When you have a child, it will be my child. And when we are all dead, that child will remain.

EMILIE
When *I* have...?

AGATHA
And that is Master Branwell's purpose.

9.

HULDEY and her diary. In the library...which is the same as the parlour. The moor rain continues.

HULDEY
(A rush of anguish.)
Monday: Agatha is awful, Emilie only ever talks to her, Emilie is uglier than I initially thought she was, and I hate Agatha.

A breath.

Tuesday: I think I'm going to kill myself.
Wednesday: If I killed myself, nobody would even notice.
Thursday—

MARJORY enters without a hat.

MARJORY
Oh. Pardon.

HULDEY
Mallory!

MARJORY
Ma'am.

HULDEY
Marjory?

MARJORY
Ma'am.

HULDEY
You've been lurking outside the Library to hear my innermost private thoughts!

MARJORY
Oh no, not at—

HULDEY
It's all right, everyone does it, sit down and I'll read to you.

Reading.

Thurs—

MARJORY

I'll just go and take care of the...

HULDEY

No! You sit there. You sit right there.
'Thursday: I had a dream about a great hulking awful man who came into my bed-chamber. I was terrified and it was terrible and I did not want him in my bed-chamber AT. ALL. and we talked for a very long time.'

To MARJORY.

You come here. Come here.

MARJORY

I'm feeling labour pains, ma'am, I think I should sit.

HULDEY

No come here. You are going to read the part of the awful man, and I am going to read the part of me, in my lacy nightgown.

MARJORY

And also my typhus is acting up again, I've been coughing blood all morning.

HULDEY

Come here RIGHT NOW.

MARJORY goes to her. HULDEY reads.

HULDEY AS HEROINE

'What can you possibly want with me, you awful man.'

MARJORY AS AWFUL MAN
(Flat monotone.)
'I cannot keep away from you.'

HULDEY AS HEROINE

'What nonsense. How horrible. What are you doing.'

MARJORY AS AWFUL MAN
(Flat monotone.)
'I am worshipping you with my eyes.'

HULDEY AS HEROINE
'That is very obscene and uncalled-for. What are you doing now?'

MARJORY AS AWFUL MAN
(Flat monotone.)
'I am worshipping you with more than my eyes.'

Beat—as herself.

Ma'am?

HULDEY
What is it.

MARJORY
(Trying to leave.)
I really have to—

HULDEY AS HEROINE
(Steam-rolling over her.)
'How brutal! How ravishing! God can see us and is judging you!'

MARJORY AS AWFUL MAN
(Flat monotone.)
'I have loved you long before you were as famous as you are currently famous. I have always wanted to know your innermost thoughts and emotions.'

HULDEY AS HEROINE
'Really?'

MARJORY AS AWFUL MAN
(Flat monotone.)
'Quite sincerely.'

HULDEY AS HEROINE
'Well. What would you like to know?'

MARJORY
(As herself.)
Why don't you kill Agatha?

A bewildered beat.
HULDEY stares at her.

HULDEY AS HEROINE

'Excuse me?'

MARJORY
(As herself.)

I said:
Why don't you kill Agatha?

> *A beat. HULDEY is completely off-balanced.*

HULDEY

Kill. Agatha?
I...
Kill? Agatha?

MARJORY

You'd be the sister who killed her sister.
A woman murderess.
The parson's daughter!
It would be shocking and horrible and nobody would be able
to stop talking about it.
You'd be infamous.

HULDEY
(Trying the word out.)

'IN...famous.'

MARJORY

It's like famous. But moreso.

HULDEY

I know what the word means. I'm an author.

MARJORY

Also, you might write about it.
What it was like to kill Agatha.
How you felt about it, before and after.

HULDEY

People always do seem to want to know those things.

MARJORY

They might want to ask you themselves.
They might want to come up here and ask you.

HULDEY

And I of course should feel very strongly about my privacy,
and wouldn't want any of that sort of vulgar crowd in my
parlour. Drinking my tea and asking me such intimate questions.

Dreaming a little.

How I feel. What it all means. Where I think I'm going in my
life next, and do I think it was because I lacked love as a child,
which of course is true, I *did* lack love as a child, what an astute
question.

MARJORY

That *is*. That *is* an astute question.

HULDEY
(Carried away by all of this.)
Did *you* lack love as a child?

MARJORY

I did, I really did.

HULDEY

Everything around here is so bleak. So loveless and bleak. And
if I were to kill Agatha—and I'm not saying I would, of course—
but if I *were*, it would sort of be a...splash of color. If you will.
A tear in the fabric.

MARJORY

Wrenching control of your life.
Of *history*.

HULDEY

History?

MARJORY

A new chapter unrolling before your eyes.
Monday: today everything changed.

HULDEY

Monday: Everything was grey and cold and then all of a sudden—
BAM!

MARJORY

Monday: 'Bam.'

HULDEY

(*A revelation!*)
They might write a song about it!

MARJORY

Sorry?

HULDEY

There are all sorts of ballads about that kind of thing.
They might write a ballad about me.

MARJORY

They might. They would.

HULDEY

Maybe if I sort of wrote my own ballad about it, that might be
the one they ended up singing all the time. So it would be like,
I'd be famous as a writer and a murderer but *also* as sort of a
singer-songwriter.

MARJORY

That sounds very likely.

HULDEY hugs her impulsively. MARJORY stands very still.

HULDEY

This is the best day I've ever had.

10.

The moors.
The MASTIFF and the MOOR-HEN.
She eats. He guards her. He's never been so at peace in the
world. Mid-conversation.

MASTIFF

… But then sometimes I think, who would I be if I weren't
depressed?
You know?
As if the thing that is making me myself is my own constant
and unyielding misery. As if happiness is some sort of altered
state, in which you're no longer quite yourself.

MOOR-HEN

What's 'depressed' again?

MASTIFF

The squashed grub.

MOOR-HEN

Oh! That's right.
Why do you want to be a squashed grub again?

MASTIFF

Forget it.

MOOR-HEN

Say it again slower.

MASTIFF

You know, it actually doesn't matter.

MOOR-HEN

It doesn't?

MASTIFF

You're here now, so it doesn't.

MOOR-HEN

That's nice.

    Reflective beat.

Is that nice?

MASTIFF

It's nice.

MOOR-HEN

Okay.

    Beat.

MASTIFF

How's your leg?

MOOR-HEN

Still hurts.

MASTIFF

Are you sure you don't want some soup? Or a blanket?

MOOR-HEN

I'm fine.

MASTIFF

Or something sweet?
Or I could pick you some flowers.

MOOR-HEN

I'm perfectly fine.

MASTIFF

Or I could make you a bed out of hay and you could sleep in it.

MOOR-HEN

I'm okay. But thank you.

MASTIFF

I just want to help. I want to do things for you.

MOOR-HEN

You're already helping.

MASTIFF

Am I?

MOOR-HEN

Well, nothing has tried to eat me while you've been here.

MASTIFF

Well that's true.

Beat.

MOOR-HEN

Why do you want to do things for me?

MASTIFF

You make me feel good.

MOOR-HEN

You told me you feel like a grub.

MASTIFF

No, that's all the times that I'm not with you.
When I'm with you, I feel like the sky is much smaller, or else
I'm much bigger, and all the things that were ready to swallow
me are now possibly weaker than I am.

MOOR-HEN
(Shy.)

When I'm with you…

She stops.

MASTIFF

What?
No what, say it.

MOOR-HEN

It's dumb.

MASTIFF

No it's not!

MOOR-HEN

You don't even know what I was going to say.

MASTIFF

It's not dumb.
Come on.

MOOR-HEN

I was just going to say…that when I'm with you…
I can't.

MASTIFF

You can!

They're both laughing.

MOOR-HEN

This is so stupid.

MASTIFF

I won't look at you.

MOOR-HEN

Okay don't look.

He looks away—in a rush:

When I'm with you I feel like the space between taking off and landing. The sort of rush. The part before everything hurts.

MASTIFF
(Very soberly.)
Do you really feel like that?

MOOR-HEN

I do.

MASTIFF

That makes me really happy.
That makes me feel like something I don't know how to describe.

MOOR-HEN
(Gently.)
It's not forever though.

MASTIFF

What do you mean?

MOOR-HEN

It's just for now. Right?

MASTIFF

What are you talking about?

MOOR-HEN

Everything is a season. The rains are a season and the cold is a season and the heat is a very short season. Everything happens and then something else happens.

MASTIFF

The way I feel about you is not a 'something else happens'.
It's an always.

MOOR-HEN

Listen.
You're wonderful.
But you're a very large dog, and your diet generally consists of...well. Things like me. And I know I'm not incredibly intelligent, and my short-term memory is—well. Short.—
But I don't really see this ending well.

MASTIFF

I would never ever hurt you.

MOOR-HEN

Every time I get up into the air, there's a moment in which all I feel is the wind rushing past me. It's very exciting and it feels very good. And I believe that it is good. But even though I intend to stay UP UP UP, the DOWN always hits eventually.

MASTIFF

This isn't like that at all.

MOOR-HEN

All I mean is...

MASTIFF
(Upset.)

This isn't gravity, this is love!

MOOR-HEN

Okay.

MASTIFF

Okay?

MOOR-HEN

Forget it.

Beat.

MASTIFF

I'll get you some hay. I'll make you a nest. And I'll take care of you. And even if it rains, you'll never get wet, and when the moor wind blows, you'll never be cold, and I will stand over you and we will be so happy. Okay?

MOOR-HEN

I guess so.

11.

MARJORY in the Portrait Gallery…which is the same room as the parlour.
She sits in the good chair. Feet up.
She is not polishing anything.
She writes in HULDEY's diary.

MARJORY

Monday: I polished.
Tuesday: I polished and I cooked.
Wednesday: I cooked more things and afterwards I scrubbed.
Thursday: It rained and Miss Emilie tracked mud everywhere and I cleaned it.
Friday: I told Huldey to murder Miss Agatha.

    Musing.

I should like to be in charge. Why should everybody else have a say but me? *I'm* the one with ideas. And my diary is full of action verbs. And if people were to ask me questions, I should have a lot more to say for myself, because I've done a lot more, I've considered a lot more, and I have a lot of thoughts about the moors and manual labour and the typhus, and also child-rearing, and if Huldey does not kill Miss Agatha soon, I shall have to murder them both, although I would much prefer someone else to do it.

    HULDEY enters.
    There is a different air about her.
    The air of a woman heading toward greatness.

HULDEY
There you are! I've been looking for you.

MARJORY
I've been here, in the Portrait Gallery.

HULDEY
Aren't you supposed to be…scrubbing? Something?

MARJORY

Every good murderess needs a confidant and a chronicler.
So right now, I am confidanting and chronicling.

HULDEY

Is that my diary?

MARJORY

No, right now this is An Historical Record. Multiple voices go
into making up An Historical Record.

HULDEY

Multiple?

MARJORY

First yours. And now mine.

HULDEY

Hm.

    Beat—on to more exciting things!

I've been working on my ballad!

MARJORY

Your what?

HULDEY

The ballad about killing Agatha.

MARJORY

… But you haven't killed her yet.

HULDEY

No, I want the ballad ready for when I do.

MARJORY

Don't you think you should be focusing on the murder?

HULDEY

I want everything ready for when it happens. I want the ballad
ready, so nobody else tries to stick their own stupid ballad in
its place, and I want to pick out the right outfit and I haven't
done that yet.

MARJORY

But how are you going to kill her?

A beat. HULDEY has not considered this.

HULDEY

Well, I don't know. I mean. People die out here all the time.

MARJORY

People *die*, but people are not *murdered*.

HULDEY

I mean there's…exposure. Isn't there? The typhus?
Complications?

MARJORY

Your sister is not ailing in the slightest.

HULDEY

Perhaps I might…uh…lure her out into the moors! 'Agatha,'
I might say, 'come outside at once!' And then she will get lost
and the quicksand will suck her under and that will be that.

*Oh dear, this could all be going terribly awry. But MARJORY
rallies.*

MARJORY
(Crafty.)
You can't put that in a ballad.

HULDEY

No?

MARJORY

No! If you're going to write a good ballad, you need a good
murder, which involves an axe or a pick or a dagger or at the
very least poison.

HULDEY

You've thought about this.

MARJORY

You haven't!

HULDEY

I have!
I have all my answers ready for when people interview me and ask me lots of questions.

MARJORY

You have *answers*?

HULDEY

Interview me! Go on! Ask me, 'Huldeygard, why did you murder your elder sister in such callous and cold blood.'

MARJORY

'Huldeygard, why / did you—'

HULDEY

I was a woman pushed to desperate straits, I tell you, desperate! Here on the moors one reaches such extremity of emotion! Now, of course, I see the error of my ways and I repent.

MARJORY

That's no good at all.

HULDEY
(Crushed.)

I thought it was rather good.

MARJORY

You can't repent! You can't see the error of your ways!

HULDEY

I can't?

MARJORY

It's BORING.

HULDEY

… Oh.

MARJORY

Nobody CARES about people who are SORRY.
Everybody FORGETS the people who are SORRY.
The only people who get remembered are the ones who are NEVER SORRY.

HULDEY takes this in. Way in.

HULDEY

Wow.

MARJORY

Just forget it. You weren't cut out for this.

HULDEY

No! No wait.

MARJORY

I have to go scrub something.

HULDEY

No wait! I can be. I can be cut out for this.

MARJORY

I don't think so. You want to be sorry and you want to be forgiven.

HULDEY

I can not want those things! I can be very cold and very brutal.

MARJORY

Can you?

HULDEY

Interview me again.

MARJORY

'Huldeygard, why did you murder your elder sister in such callous and cold blood.'

HULDEY
(Coldly and with poise.)
Because that is what I am, sir. A murderess.

Beat. Okay. Better.

MARJORY

'And how do you feel in the aftermath?'

HULDEY

Nothing.

                              MARJORY
'Nothing?'

                              HULDEY
I feel nothing.

    Beat.

                              MARJORY
That was okay.

                              HULDEY
Was it good?

                              MARJORY
It was better.

                              HULDEY
It was good, wasn't it.

                              MARJORY
You *are* going to do it, aren't you?

                              HULDEY
Of course.

                              MARJORY
Of course?

                              HULDEY
Of course I'm going to do it!

                              MARJORY
Okay.
When?

                              HULDEY
What?

                              MARJORY
I said: When. Are you going to do it?

    Beat.

HULDEY

Well. Soon.

Beat.

MARJORY

Someone else might do it first. If you didn't.

HULDEY

What?!

MARJORY

I'm just saying. It's an opportunity. Everybody wants opportunity. So if you didn't take this one, someone else might do it, and then you wouldn't be anything, really. You'd just be sad old Huldey alone in the house on the moors. Sad sad Huldey, whose sister got killed by someone else, which would get you a little pity, I guess, a sympathy vote, but nobody likes to think about victims, it makes them feel sad, so eventually nobody would like to think about you. At all. Ever.

A beat. HULDEY stands with new-found conviction.

HULDEY

Nobody is going to murder my sister before I do.

She marches from the room.
MARJORY watches her go.

12.

AGATHA's bed-chamber. Which appears to be the same room as the parlour. AGATHA sits in a very uncomfortable chair. She reads EMILIE's letters to herself.

AGATHA

Ah.

> *Reads.*

Yes.

> *Reads—corrects the spelling.*

With an 'A,' Emilie, not an 'I'.

> *Reads.*

Not bad.

> *At a sound nearby:*

Yes?

> *EMILIE steps into the light.*

EMILIE

May I?

AGATHA

It is very late. It is very late to be slipping into people's bedrooms.

EMILIE

I know.

AGATHA

Come in.

> *EMILIE does. Looking around.*

EMILIE

Your bedroom is very...spare.

AGATHA

Yes.
Will you have a night cap?

EMILIE
(A little shocked.)

Do you drink?

AGATHA

Do you find it unladylike?

EMILIE

Of course.

AGATHA

Good.

> *She produces a flask. Offers it. EMILIE takes it and sips. Then returns to AGATHA.*

So...why have you come at this hour?

EMILIE

I had to see you.

AGATHA
(But gently.)
Impulse is not the same thing as courage.

EMILIE

Neither is liquor.

AGATHA
(Toasting slightly.)
A fair point.

> *A beat.*

EMILIE

I have thought about it. What you're asking.
It would once have been unthinkable.

AGATHA

But now it is not?

EMILIE

When we were out on the moors...everything was...endless.
And some might call it unforgiving. Bleak. Terrifying, even.

My eyes saw it that way at first. But as we stood there I began to see it as you did. As a place of…power, perhaps. A place that belonged to itself. And I wondered…what it would be, to belong to a place like that.

AGATHA

Did you.

EMILIE

I've moved from house to house my whole life. There's always a lady of the house who can't abide me, a gentleman of the house who pursues me, a child who dies of something awful— and then I move on. Wherever I go, it is all the same, and I'm always a stranger. What you showed me…it has a strong pull.

AGATHA

'However'?

EMILIE

However.
A young girl, unprotected, requires certain assurances.

AGATHA
(Surprised and interested.)

'Assurances'.

EMILIE

You understand.

AGATHA

We'll see if I do. Go on.

EMILIE

My child will be the heir to all of this. Is that not right?

AGATHA

My child.

EMILIE

… *Our* child.

AGATHA
(Acknowledges: term one.)

…will be the heir, yes.

EMILIE

And this child will need a firm and guiding hand. From its mother, who must be nearby.

AGATHA

'Nearby'?

EMILIE
(Direct.)
My own wing and my own servant.

AGATHA

One room, near the nursery. Mallory will be your servant.

EMILIE

My own wing, and Mallory won't do.

AGATHA

Two rooms, in the west wing. Mallory will be instructed to behave better toward you.

EMILIE

Two rooms, in perpetuity. I can handle Mallory myself.

AGATHA

In *perpetuity*?

EMILIE

If I give this family an heir, I give it life. By my calculation, that makes me a member.

A beat, and then AGATHA smiles.

AGATHA

I am so rarely surprised. But how enjoyable when it occurs.

EMILIE

… Thank you.

AGATHA

I have chosen well, and you will perform satisfactorily, and that makes me…content.

EMILIE

I'd like to make you happy.

AGATHA

I believe the word I used was 'content'.
Well. Shall we shake on it?

Beat.

EMILIE

And then there is the matter of...what lies between us.

AGATHA

Excuse me?

EMILIE

Have I surprised you again?

AGATHA

Twice in one night is a little much.

EMILIE

I see the way you look at me. And when you see that I see,
and you become cold—that doesn't escape my notice either.

AGATHA

I can't imagine what you're referring to.

EMILIE

You wanted a sweet young governess and you summoned one,
that's true. But out on the moors, it wasn't just a governess you
wanted. It was me.

A beat. AGATHA is—can it be?—a little uncomfortable.

AGATHA

Is this...conversation...a necessary part of our negotiation?

EMILIE

What assurances can you offer, regarding us?

AGATHA

There are rarely assurances to be had, in such matters.

EMILIE

No?

AGATHA

None that can be believed.

EMILIE

I disagree.

A beat.

AGATHA
(Genuine.)

Are you in love, little Emilie?

EMILIE

I've never felt the way I felt when I read your letters.
I've never felt that way in my whole life.

AGATHA

And when you see me face to face, and I am nothing like the
man in your letters?

EMILIE

On the contrary, you are very much like him.

AGATHA

How is that?

EMILIE

The man in the letters was merciless, and you are merciless.
He was overly bold, and your eyes are bold. He doled out
kindness sparingly so I was hungry for it, and this is what you
do as well, I know you are doing it and yet I still find myself
willing to do almost anything for a moment of that kindness.
The man in the letters was a strategist, Agatha, and that is
exactly what you are.

AGATHA is surprised, despite herself.

AGATHA

That was remarkably astute of you.

EMILIE

You thought I was stupid.

AGATHA

Educated, of course, but quite stupid.

EMILIE

And how do you feel about me now?

A beat between them. AGATHA smiles.

AGATHA

Come sit with me.

EMILIE does.

You have made a fair number of orthographical mistakes in your letters. I have circled them for you so that you may see.

EMILIE
(Nonplussed.)
You have...circled my mistakes?

AGATHA

If one can see one's mistakes plain in the face, one does not repeat them. Does one.

She looks EMILIE plain in the face.
Very close. Within kissing distance.
Giving EMILIE space to decide.

EMILIE

This is no mistake.

EMILIE kisses her. AGATHA gives in to the kiss. When it ends...

And there it is... How you're looking at me.

AGATHA

Emilie...

EMILIE

If I love you, don't mistake that for weakness.
What I'll love most is what you have to offer.

AGATHA

Very good.

EMILIE

Is it?

AGATHA

There is nothing in this world more honest and dependable than self-interest.

Beat.

When the clock strikes midnight, you may go upstairs to Branwell. Until then, put your head in my lap and rest.

EMILIE leans back against AGATHA. She produces HULDEY's diary.

EMILIE

This was left in the Solarium tonight.
It was left open, and I saw my name.

AGATHA

How appalling.

EMILIE

Don't you want to know what she says about us?

AGATHA

I seek to never concern myself with the inner life of my sister.

EMILIE
(Reading.)

Monday: Emilie does nothing but stare at Agatha, do I even exist, I hate Agatha.
Tuesday: if I were to die and return in a different form, I should like to be a rat, because their lives are much much shorter.
Wednesday: Bam!

Still reading, but surprised.

Today is the best // day—

AGATHA
(Takes the diary, closes it.)
Enough.

EMILIE
All right then, sing me a lullaby.

AGATHA
A lullaby!

EMILIE
I am always the one singing lullabies to children who hate me.
This may be my only opportunity to have one sung to me.

AGATHA
(With unaccustomed gentleness.)
I don't know any lullabies. I have never sung one.

EMILIE
What you do is, you think of some very simple words.
And you sing them to a very simple tune.

Beat. AGATHA thinks hard. Then she sings to EMILIE. Her voice is rusty and a little awful but also strangely touching. She uses the melody that EMILIE sang before.

AGATHA
Good night Emilie
Soon you will visit Branwell in the attic
He is up in the attic
But then you will come back down
And it will be very nice
Your bones and blood will be part of this land
And they'll bury you here when you die.

13.

The MASTIFF and the MOOR-HEN.
It's late at night.
He's made her a nest of straw.
She sits in it, sort of awkwardly.
The MASTIFF has been talking for a long time.

MASTIFF

—and usually that makes me feel alienated and cut-off
but this time, I just thought it was beautiful
a little romantic, actually
and then I thought: I would do anything for you.

    Beat.

What are you thinking?

MOOR-HEN

My leg is a lot better.

MASTIFF

Oh that's wonderful!

    Beat.

How better?

MOOR-HEN

A lot better. I can stand. I can walk.

MASTIFF

Oh.

MOOR-HEN

What do you mean Oh?

MASTIFF

Nothing.

MOOR-HEN

What.

MASTIFF

It's good that you can stand and that you can walk.

But if you can stand and you can walk, maybe you can walk away from me.

Beat.

MOOR-HEN
But right now I'm sitting and resting.

MASTIFF
Okay.

MOOR-HEN
Right now we're both just sitting and resting.

Beat.

MASTIFF
I was thinking, what if I learned to fly?

MOOR-HEN
To...fly?

MASTIFF
Yes, what if I learned how to do it too, and then you could fly away if you wanted, but I could go with you, and if you crash-landed again I could help you, or also maybe if I was with you, you wouldn't crash-land.

The MOOR-HEN gives this serious thought.

MOOR-HEN
You? Fly?

MASTIFF
Me fly.

MOOR-HEN
I don't think you can fly.
Can you?

MASTIFF
I've never tried.

MOOR-HEN

I don't think... I mean. I'm not very educated. But I don't think
I've ever seen that before.

MASTIFF

I'd do it for you. If you wanted me to.

MOOR-HEN

Let me think about that.

MASTIFF

Do you not want me to go with you? Do you not want me with
you all the time?

MOOR-HEN

Well maybe not *all* the time.
I mean.
There's privacy.

MASTIFF

I hate privacy. Everything is always already private anyway.
I want to be so close to you that it feels like my skin is going
to explode.

Beat.

MOOR-HEN

Maybe you could fly a little bit behind me, sometimes.
So you could still see me, but I'd have privacy.

MASTIFF

I guess I could do that.

Beat—sad.

I don't think I can fly.

Beat—tentative.

Maybe you could not fly.

MOOR-HEN

What?

MASTIFF

Maybe you could not fly.

MOOR-HEN

Not...fly.

MASTIFF

Maybe—I don't know, I'm just bouncing ideas around here—
Maybe you could just kind of. Walk. From now on.
And I could walk next to you.

MOOR-HEN

Walk?
I'm bad at walking.
I limp.

MASTIFF

Or I could walk a step or two behind you, but if you stumbled
at all, I'd catch you immediately.

MOOR-HEN

Wait a minute...

MASTIFF

Or actually, if you sat in a little wagon? With wheels? I could
push you.
So you wouldn't have to walk.

MOOR-HEN

But what if I wanted to?

MASTIFF

If you wanted to walk, you could walk.

MOOR-HEN

But what if I wanted to fly?

Beat.

MASTIFF is depressed but also upset.
Even if he tries to keep a lid on it.

MASTIFF

I just don't understand why you'd want to do something I couldn't do when there are lots of other things you could do that I *can* do. Unless you haven't been happy with me. Have you not been happy?

MOOR-HEN

That's not what I'm saying.

MASTIFF
(Losing it a little.)
Then I don't understand what you're saying. Because you hate flying! So if you are wanting to do something that I can't do, that you hate, it must be because you want to get away from me!

MOOR-HEN

I just. I am something. That flies. That's all.

MASTIFF

Sorry.
I'm sorry.
I don't mean to be crazy.
You just
you mean so much
you have no idea.

MOOR-HEN

I'm not saying you're crazy. But it freaks me out when you get intense.

MASTIFF

Sorry, I'm sorry.

MOOR-HEN

Don't be sorry, just be calm.

MASTIFF

Okay.
Calm. Okay.

> *Beat—an outburst again.*

I just, I have this nightmare where I turn my back for a second and then I feel this *tug*, inside me somewhere inside my heart somewhere, and I turn around but it's too late, you're *rising* into the sky, you're just drifting away from me and I can't reach you and you won't come back down and all I can do is watch you get smaller and smaller and smaller until the moors have swallowed you completely and you're gone.

Beat.

MOOR-HEN

I'm right here.

MASTIFF

Now. You're right here *now.*

MOOR-HEN

I am right here. Now.

MASTIFF

What about tomorrow?

MOOR-HEN

You're getting intense again.

MASTIFF

Sorry.
Sorry.

Beat.

I don't ever want to feel the way I felt before I met you.

MOOR-HEN

But sometimes you will. Sometimes you will feel like that.

MASTIFF

Not if you don't fly away from me!

MOOR-HEN

Even if I don't fly away from you, there will be a moment in which you look at my face, and it isn't the face you thought you were looking at, maybe it has an expression that you don't recognise. Or you'll hear something about my past that you didn't know, that will make you wonder if you really know me. And then, for that time, for however long it lasts, you will feel like a squashed grub again.

Beat. MASTIFF really looks at her.

MASTIFF

Then you should tell me everything about yourself now. And I'll learn all your expressions. And then I'll never feel that way.

MOOR-HEN

I don't think you're really hearing what I'm saying.

MASTIFF

Come here. Sit very close to me and tell me everything.

MOOR-HEN

Actually. I'd like to be here. And you can be there. And maybe we can be quiet for a little bit.

MASTIFF

I can feel you drifting away. I can feel a distance between us. Why is there a distance between us?

MOOR-HEN

Because sometimes there is a distance. Because this is a place built on distance. And that's okay.

MASTIFF

It's horrible. I feel horrible. Hold onto me.

MOOR-HEN

Breathe.
Okay?
Take deep breaths.
Count.
Breathe in the shape of a square.
Calm down.

The MASTIFF calms down.
When he's calm he looks at her.
New determination. Almost scary.

MASTIFF

I won't let it happen.

MOOR-HEN

What?

MASTIFF

I won't let you drift away from me.

14.

The Great Hall...which looks the same as the parlour. Late that same night. AGATHA is alone, waiting for EMILIE to return from the attic. Perhaps she paces. Perhaps she sits.

HULDEY enters. She's dressed unusually well. She carries a small axe behind her back. She keeps it out of sight of AGATHA at all times.

HULDEY

There you are!

AGATHA

You. **HULDEY**

I've been looking for you. And here you are, in the Great Hall.

AGATHA

I should think you would be asleep.

HULDEY

I should think *you* would be asleep.

Beat.

Where have you been all evening?

AGATHA

I was feeling...unwell.

HULDEY

And where has Emilie been?

AGATHA

I imagine Miss Vandergaard was also feeling...unwell.

Beat.

Were you playing dress-up?

HULDEY

Why can't you just say that I look nice?

AGATHA

If I meant to say that you looked nice, I would have said that
you looked nice.

Beat.

HULDEY

One of my diaries has gone missing tonight.

AGATHA

Oh?

HULDEY

I looked for it everywhere, I couldn't find it.

AGATHA

You must have misplaced it.

HULDEY watches her, clutching her axe.

HULDEY

Sister.

AGATHA

Yes, sister.

HULDEY

I am very. very. unhappy.

AGATHA

Is that so.

HULDEY

Yes it is, it is so now, and it has always been so.

AGATHA

That doesn't make you special.

HULDEY

… What?

AGATHA

Everybody is very very unhappy, Huldey. It is simply what
things are. The land is bleak and the house is large and there
is no language for all the things lurking within us, no matter

how much we write in our diaries, and we are all quite unhappy. So what.

> *Beat. HULDEY didn't expect this.*
> *She might lower or put down the axe, which AGATHA still has not seen.*

HULDEY

Are *you*...unhappy?

AGATHA

I have achieved balance.

HULDEY

Balance?

AGATHA

I do not strive for happiness. Which has made me less unhappy. I set goals for myself, and I achieve those goals.
You might try it, if you weren't scribbling in your diary all the time.

HULDEY

But what if... I mean. Aren't there. Other ways?

AGATHA

And what would those 'other ways' be?

HULDEY

If something amazing happened. Something wild or spectacular or completely unexpected. Don't you think it would make us happy?

> *The briefest of beats. And then:*

AGATHA

No.

HULDEY

Why not?

AGATHA

Because then that event would be over. The wild, spectacular— whatever it was. And then you would be alone again, only this time you would not have achieved balance, you would have achieved expectation. You would want to feel that way again and again, more and more, and you would *not* feel that way again and again more and more, and so you would be. even. more. unhappy.

Now the axe has definitely been put down.

HULDEY
(But not meanly—almost searchingly.)
I think I hate you.

AGATHA
I know that.

HULDEY
You do?

AGATHA
I read your diary.

HULDEY
(A little delighted.)
You did?

AGATHA
I did.

HULDEY
And what did you think of it?

AGATHA
I thought it was of very poor quality.

HULDEY is crushed.

HULDEY
You…did?

AGATHA
I am sorry to say that I did.

HULDEY
And…why? Why did you feel that way?

AGATHA

There was monotony, repetition, poor attention to detail, a plaintive narrator's voice that did little to endear itself with the reader, your spelling could improve immensely—to be honest I'm shocked that it hasn't—but mostly, to be candid, it was boring.

HULDEY
(White-faced.)

Boring?

AGATHA

Quite quite
boring.

> *A beat.*
> *And then HULDEY launches herself at AGATHA.*
> *This was entirely unplanned.*
> *She is fueled by sheer rage and hurt.*
> *She hits AGATHA in the head with a heavy object. Perhaps a vase? Not the axe.*
> *AGATHA falls.*
> *HULDEY keeps hitting her, blind with rage.*

HULDEY

I
AM
NOT
BORING!!!!
I
AM
FAMOUS!
I
AM
SO
FAMOUS!
I
HAVE
A
SONG!!
ABOUT
ME!

NOBODY
ELSE
HERE
HAS
A
SONG!

> *Beat. She looks at AGATHA.*
> *AGATHA is quite dead.*
> *HULDEY has no idea what to do.*

... Agatha?
Agatha.
Agatha?

> *A beat.*

> *There's blood all over her.*
> *She's shaking.*

Oh.
Well.
Oh.

> *She has no idea what to do.*

Marjory?
Mallory!
Marjory!!
Mallory!!

> *Nobody comes. She has no idea.*

Oh!
Well.
I am going to sing my song now.

> *Beat.*

> *This starts off melodiously sung.*
> *Then turns into a crazy rock power ballad.*
> *Fog and lights and blood and madness.*

HULDEY'S POWER BALLAD

There's a haunting wind on the moors tonight
There's a blood-red moon so bold
They'll all build fires in their hearths tonight
But mine alone stands cold.
There's a driving rain on the moors tonight
Fragile hawks and little hares must hide
There's a biting cold in the air tonight
But I alone don't mind.
Murder is a colour like the heat of the day
Murder is the gentleman you wish would stay
Murder is the orange dress you thought you couldn't afford
A murderess, you know, is never bored.
Murder is a colour like the deepest summer sky
Murder is a baby bird who suddenly learned to fly
Murder is a woman's most prestigious award
And a murderess, I say, is never bored.
I did a thing, a very bad thing
I chopped her head with one great swing
I beat her dead 'til she was gory
… I'm not sorry
I did a thing, a very bad thing
I chopped her head with one great swing
I beat her dead 'til she was gory
… I'm not sorry

Rap section.

The axe went whack and then her skull went crick-a-crack-crack
here's a drippy-drip as her blood goes split-a-splat-splat
and cree-cree-CREE goes the owl in the dark of night
whoo-whoo WHO will come for you, it's you-know-who: a
murderess is nigh!

Singing again.

I did a thing, a very bad thing
I chopped her head with one great swing
I beat her dead 'til she was gory
… I'm not sorry!!

HULDEY reaches the end of it.
A sea of applause crashes over her.
It is the sweetest sound she has ever heard.
It nourishes her like sunlight to a starving plant. She bathes in it. Slowly, the applause filters away. Slowly, we start to hear rain instead, and wild wind. There is no applause. There is a storm outside. HULDEY doesn't feel this shift at first.

HULDEY

Thank you
thank you
yes I am
yes I did
yes and I feel nothing
Oh it means so much to see you all here tonight
thank you, thank you…

Feeling the shift.

Wait.
Wait.
Where did you go?
Come back!

She opens the door and rain drives in.
She dashes out onto the moors and is devoured by them.

15

The Great Hall...which continues to look very much like the parlour. Next morning. A gigantic blood stain on the floor. MARJORY's diary sits on AGATHA's chair.

EMILIE stands in front of the bloodstain. She has just entered. She stares at it, in horror. The sound of someone coming. EMILIE sits down in the chair, diary in hand, and composes her face. MARJORY enters with a mop and bucket.

MARJORY

Oh.

EMILIE

Mallory.

MARJORY

I didn't know anyone was in here.

EMILIE

I'm in here.

MARJORY

I can see that.

Beat—staring at the stain.

I was just going to...dust.

EMILIE

Were you?

MARJORY

The Great Hall has fallen into...disarray.

EMILIE

Oh, I hadn't noticed.

A beat between them. MARJORY puts the mop and bucket aside.

MARJORY

I can see you found my diary.

EMILIE

Is this your diary?

MARJORY

It is.

EMILIE

I thought it was Huldey's diary.

MARJORY

It was Huldey's diary and then it became my diary.

EMILIE

Oh.

A beat.

MARJORY

Have you seen Miss Huldey this morning?

EMILIE

I?

MARJORY

Yes.

EMILIE

No.
No doubt she's taking a long walk on the moors.

MARJORY

No doubt.

EMILIE

Are you looking for her?

MARJORY

No, not I.

EMILIE

Have you seen Miss Agatha?

MARJORY

No, I can't say that I have.
Why, are you looking for her?

EMILIE

I? No no.

MARJORY

Are you sure?

EMILIE

I'm quite content, thank you.
I have no need of either.

A beat between them.

MARJORY

You look different.

EMILIE

I do?

MARJORY

Somehow you do.

EMILIE

Well. Isn't that something.

Beat.

MARJORY

You might read out loud.

EMILIE

But it's your diary, Mallory, you know what it says.

MARJORY

Margaret.

EMILIE

Excuse me?

MARJORY

I'm 'Margaret'. When I'm an author.

EMILIE

Oh.

Reads out loud.

'Monday: Everything shall always be different now. And yet nothing changes in this bleak land. I once saw a kitten ripped apart by savage birds. It seemed that such an awful thing would change the face of the land forever. And yet, when it was over, there was no sign that it had occurred, save a little bit of fur caught in the gorse.'

To MARJORY.

Quite good, Margaret, really.

MARJORY

That's very kind.

EMILIE

Did that actually happen?

MARJORY

Oh. I'm not sure. It's hard to tell.

EMILIE

I understand perfectly.
You might say a 'scrap' of fur.

MARJORY

'Scrap'?

EMILIE

It's a better word than 'bit'.

MARJORY

'Save a little scrap of fur'.
Oh. That is better.

EMILIE

The alliteration, you see.

MARJORY

Yes, that's nice.

> *The door opens. Both women look.*
> *The MASTIFF walks in.*
> *He is covered in blood.*
> *Feathers stuck to the blood.*

He walks straight past them and goes to sit by the fire. He stares blankly into the fire.

EMILIE

What on earth has happened to the dog.

MARJORY

It must have gone hunting, I imagine.

EMILIE

It must have caught something.

MARJORY

I suppose it must.

EMILIE

Sit down, Margaret. Here's a pen.
Read it all again, and let us make some judicious alterations.

*MARJORY takes the pen. She takes the diary.
She sits. EMILIE watches her keenly.*

MARJORY

Monday: Everything shall always be different now. And yet nothing changes—

EMILIE

Oh yes.
That's good.
That's very good.

Blackout.

End of play.

SCORE

Score

Agatha's Lullaby

for THE MOORS

1/18/2016

Silverman

Kluger

as though improvised

Good ni - ght,_____ Good ni - ght, Em - i - lie._____

p

_____ Soon you will vi - sit Bran - well in the att - ic.

cantabile

He is up in the att - ic._____ But then you will come back down.

mp

And it will be ver - y nice. Oh, it will be ver - y nice. Yes,

mp

broadly, significantly

it will be ver - y nice. Your bones and blood will be part of this land

pppp   *mp*   *subito p*

And they'll bur - y you here when you die.

ppp

EMILIE'S SONG

(from The Moors)

VOICE + TAB (Lute: GCEA)

music by DAN KLUGER
words by JEN SILVERMAN

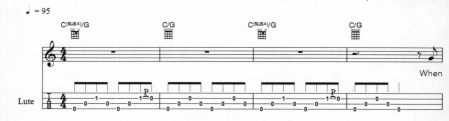

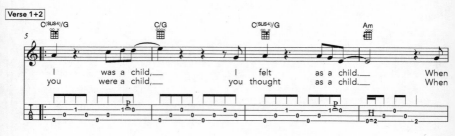

Music Preparation by Lee Kinney

EMILIE'S SONG

THE MOORS - power ballad
rev 9/12/2015

Kluger

THE MOORS - power ballad

THE MOORS - power ballad

I'm not sorr-y. I did a thing, a ver-y bad thing I chopped her head with one great swing I cut her up and earned my glor-y

I'm not sorr - y.

THE ROOMMATE

This play is for Laurel Laffrey

THE ROOMMATE premiered at Actors Theatre of Louisville's Humana Festival in Spring 2015 under the artistic leadership of Les Waters. It was directed by Mike Donahue, set design by Andrew Boyce, costumes by Kathleen Geldard, lighting by Paul Toben, music and sound by Daniel Kluger, and dramaturgy by Kimberly Colburn. The cast was as follows:

ROBYN	Tasha Lawrence
SHARON	Margaret Daly

THE ROOMMATE was further developed, and produced with a different ending at Williamstown Theatre Festival in Summer 2017, under the artistic leadership of Mandy Greenfield. It was directed by Mike Donahue, set design by Dane Laffrey, costumes by Anita Yavitch, lighting by Scott Zielinski, and sound by Stowe Nelson. The cast was as follows:

ROBYN	Jane Kaczmarek
SHARON	S. Epatha Merkerson

***

A real debt of thanks to the many theaters that produced this play as it grew and changed. Personal thanks to Les Waters, Meredith McDonough, Amy Wegener, and Kimberly Colburn, who took a risk on a first draft; to Mike Donahue and Dane Laffrey, who helped me co-parent this play from its earliest stages; and to Mandy Greenfield, who gave us the chance to dig back in, the benefit of her sharp dramaturgical insights, and the trust that we'd figure it out in the end.

CAST

SHARON   F, 54.

ROBYN   F, 56.

TIME

Now.
Summer.

PLACE

A big old house in Iowa City.

NOTES ON THE TEXT

On line breaks: The spacing is a gesture toward indicating rhythm and how thoughts change, morph, contradict each other, escalate, or get supplanted by other thoughts as we talk. Line breaks often signal either an intensification of, or a shift away, from something. They do <u>not</u> indicate a beat or pause except where written.

On punctuation: Sections of dialogue may sometimes end without punctuation. When this happens, this is a gesture toward the fluidity and energy of the exchanges. The difference between a sentence that ends with a period and one without is very slight—often the difference lies in the breath.

On casting: This play welcomes diverse casting in any number of combinations. However, having Sharon played by a White actor and Robyn played by a Black actor will replicate certain worn racial tropes that this play does not intend. Please avoid that particular combination in your casting. (The reverse, however, can work quite well.)

On tone: The play is often funny, but don't think of it as a pure comedy. The humor comes from a dark and often lonely place, which keeps Sharon's escalating choices from feeling like absurdist flourishes. The second the play tips into 'broadness' or 'farce' it loses its heart.

On music: The song on Sharon's CD in Scene 3 might be Mary Chapin Carpenter's 'Transcendental Reunion'. New Music at the end of Scene 3 might be Patti Smith's 'Dancing Barefoot'. And 'World War II London Music' might be Sydney Bechet's track 'Si Tu Vois Ma Mére'.

[ ] is unspoken, although the character is thinking it.

( ) is spoken out loud but is a side thought.

1.

The kitchen.

SHARON finishes helping ROBYN carry boxes in. So many boxes!
One contains weird vegetables from a CSA. Some vegetables
are just odd, but others look actively dangerous.

SHARON
(A little out of breath.)
And this is the kitchen
I'm a big cook, I love to cook
You said you cooked?

ROBYN

I cook, sure.

SHARON

Okay! Okay
Well
we can divide up the refrigerator or the pantry shelves
depending on
sort of *what* and *when* you cook

ROBYN

I'm a vegan

SHARON
(Doesn't really know what that is.)
Okay! Okay…

ROBYN

No animal products.

SHARON

Okay!
So like…no meat…

ROBYN

Nope, no meat

SHARON

Or eggs

                    ROBYN

That would be an animal product

                    SHARON

Sure! Sure it would
Uh...but like, carrots

                    ROBYN

Yes carrots are fine

                    SHARON

I mean, clearly carrots are [fine]
...but for example, using pans or pots or
knives or
you know, that I've used for meat...
I mean, is that going to be...?

                    ROBYN

I have my own cooking utensils
in one of the boxes there's

                    SHARON

Oh! sure sure
yeah we can find
there's some extra cabinet space if we just
move things around a bit

                    ROBYN

Yeah there's a lot of space
this seems very spacious

                    SHARON

I mean there's *space*
it's not *palatial* but
I mean, Iowa, it specializes in
corn and *space*

    She laughs, ROBYN doesn't. Awkward.

If you want you can leave stuff on the porch
'til you're all unpacked

ROBYN

Oh no no, I don't want to take up your

SHARON

No no! that's fine
I don't use the side porch that much anyway
it's nice in the summer I guess but

Picking up weird vegetable:

What's this?

ROBYN

That's goya.

SHARON

What-now?

ROBYN

Goya. It's a vegetable.
A bitter gourd.

SHARON

Okay! yes. yes. Wow. Well. I see I am going to learn a lot from
having you as a roommate.

She laughs. ROBYN doesn't really.

Beat.

SHARON

You must be tired. Driving all the way from… New York, you said?

ROBYN

The Bronx.

SHARON

The—! The Bronx!

ROBYN

Took about two days, by car.

SHARON

I thought…

ROBYN
What?

SHARON
I don't know,
When you said New York, I thought
somewhere Upstate
I didn't think...
Isn't The Bronx...
dangerous?

ROBYN
'Dangerous'.

SHARON
And you're—I mean. You're a woman.
I mean. I don't know.
I've never lived in New York.

ROBYN
It's OK. I mean. There's parts. Parts where you don't wanna,
late at night, you don't wanna
but it's fine. I stayed there for a little while and nothing ever

SHARON
(With relief.)
Oh you aren't *from* the Bronx!

  A slight pause.

ROBYN
Everywhere has parts like that.

SHARON
Oh it's mostly pretty safe here.
Except for the tornados.

ROBYN
(Alarmed.)
Tornados?

SHARON
Oh yeah, in the spring mostly

early summer
you just go on down to the basement 'til they pass. It's fine.

ROBYN
(Even more alarmed.)
There are a lot of tornados here?

SHARON
Not as bad as some places.

ROBYN
Like how many tornados would you say, on average?

SHARON
It's fine! If you hear that big old siren
you just go down to the basement.
Really
it's no scarier than the Bronx.

ROBYN
(Has to smile.)
I guess not if you're from here.

SHARON
(Immediately.)
I'm not *from* here. You know. I'm not *Iowan.*

ROBYN
Oh OK

SHARON
I don't know if I said that?
when we talked on the phone, if I said that?

ROBYN
I don't think so, but it doesn't really

SHARON
I'm from Illinois, originally.

ROBYN
Oh!

SHARON

It's actually quite different from Iowa.

ROBYN

I'll take your word for it.

    Beat.

SHARON

My son lives in New York.

ROBYN

Oh!
You have a son?

SHARON

I do, he lives in New York.

ROBYN

That's great. In the Bronx?

SHARON

No! No no
He lives
'Park Slope' do you know where [that is?]
He lives in 'Park Slope'.

ROBYN

Oh yeah, that's great.

SHARON

He pays way too much for [rent]
I tell him that all the time, I say
In Iowa you could have a *house* for the money you spend on [rent]

    Laughs a little, stops.

He doesn't like it when I say that.
He didn't like Iowa.

ROBYN

The tornados?

SHARON

No he just didn't like it.

Beat. Have they run out of conversation? SHARON hastens.

He's a designer.

ROBYN

Oh! That's great!

SHARON

He's very good, everybody thinks he's very good.

ROBYN

What does he design?

SHARON
(Doesn't really know.)
Clothes, he mostly designs clothes. For women?

ROBYN

Oh!

SHARON

Everybody thinks he's a homosexual, but he's not.

Where did this come from?? SHARON has surprised herself. A beat.

ROBYN

I'm gay.

SHARON

Oh!
You're—?
Oh!!
You're—??

Beat.

I mean, I don't have any problem with homosexuals.

ROBYN

Oh good.

SHARON

Nope. Not at all. I think, you know, gay rights! Let them marry!

ROBYN

Thank you.

SHARON

Some of my son's friends are homosexual people. Probably most of them.

ROBYN

Oh.

SHARON

I think most New Yorkers are.

ROBYN

I think actually there are a lot of straight people in New York.

SHARON

I kissed a girl once in college.

Beat.

I'm sorry. I'm nervous.

ROBYN

Why are you nervous?

SHARON

I mean. A roommate! I've never had a roommate.

This is an admission of failure:

I'm fifty-four years old.
A roommate!

ROBYN

It's OK. You'll save money.

SHARON

No, I know! I know. I definitely
I will definitely save money.

Beat.

You—did you have a lot more boxes in the car?

ROBYN

I've got it.

SHARON
(Really doesn't want to keep carrying boxes.)
Well if you're sure.

ROBYN

Be right back.

She exits back out to the car.

SHARON sits alone in her kitchen with all these new weird vegetables. She takes a deep breath. OK. It's OK.

SHARON
(Calling after her.)
Today is my reading group!

ROBYN
(Offstage.)

What did you say?

SHARON

Oh, I said: today is my reading group.
If you want to come with me.

ROBYN returns. She's carrying a heavy box.

ROBYN

Your 'reading group'?

SHARON

You know, a book club. Only Tanya calls it a reading group—

She jumps up to help ROBYN set the box on the table. ROBYN pulls away.

ROBYN

I've got it!

SHARON

—Tanya's the one who runs it, she says everything just a little bit wrong, it's because she's from Idaho and there wasn't any culture there, so she didn't get exposed to things until much later in life.

Beat.

Is that more vegetables?

ROBYN

No that goes upstairs.
A reading group...

Beat.

Isn't that. Kind of. For old people?

SHARON
(Amazed.)

We *are* old people.

ROBYN
(Amazed.)

We are?

A beat. They study each other.
Each is kind of baffled by the other.
Then ROBYN turns away.

ROBYN

I'll just take this upstairs. But thanks for the invitation.

SHARON

You're so welcome. You let me know if there's anything you need. Mi casa es su casa!

Beat.

Literally.

ROBYN

OK then.

She picks up the box and almost drops it.
A ceramic doll falls out and smashes.
The box is full of ceramic dolls.

SHARON

Oh no!

ROBYN

Stay there!

ROBYN moves quickly between SHARON and the shards.

SHARON

Are you OK? Do you need help?

ROBYN
(Sharp.)

I've got this!
Is there a [broom]?

SHARON

Here…

Gets her a broom.

Do you want me to…?

ROBYN

No no
I've got it.

As she sweeps—calmer.

Sorry. I didn't mean to [snap]
I just didn't want you to get cut.

SHARON
(Peering into the box.)
What…are all these dolls?

ROBYN

Please!!

SHARON moves away from the box.

Sorry. They're—it's personal.

SHARON

I didn't mean to pry.

ROBYN

I made them. I used to be a potter.

SHARON

You were?

ROBYN

They're patterned after these antique South American dolls.

SHARON

Oh! Wow

ROBYN

But then I stopped. So.
It's a little embarrassing.

SHARON

You shouldn't be embarrassed, they're very

She doesn't like them.

Evocative.

ROBYN

Evocative?

SHARON

They evoke things.

ROBYN

They're actually voodoo dolls.

SHARON

Voodoo??

ROBYN

Kidding.

SHARON

I mean I don't know
They look a little voodoo-y to me.

ROBYN

Maybe they *evoke* voodoo.

A beat. They share a smile.

SHARON

I didn't mean that in a bad way.

ROBYN

It's OK. I'm done with all that.

SHARON

Why did you stop?

ROBYN

I stopped because
uh
it wasn't the sort of lifestyle
that...
Being a potter can be very
stressful.

Beat.

SHARON

Your boxes are so heavy and you just got here.
Leave them on the porch and put your feet up.
I'll get us coffee.

ROBYN

Is your porch safe?

SHARON

Safe?

ROBYN

Break ins?

SHARON

This is Iowa.

THE ROOMMATE

ROBYN

Yes?

SHARON

No break ins.

ROBYN

But you lock the doors?

SHARON

I *can* lock the doors.
If that makes you feel comfortable, I can *start* locking the doors.

ROBYN

I feel better with things. Locked.

SHARON

A New York thing?

ROBYN

Sure.

SHARON

A Bronx thing?

ROBYN

A Robyn thing.

> *Re: the doll box.*

I'll just take this up to my room…

SHARON

Oh! just up the stairs
immediate left—
would you like me to show you?

ROBYN

I've got it.
Here we go, take two.

> *She hoists the box with the dolls and exits upstairs.*

2.

Morning. Kitchen.

SHARON on the phone with her son.

SHARON
(Excited, sotto voce.)

And here's the other thing!
She's a homosexual!

Beat.

Well I don't care OF COURSE, but you asked if anything
interesting happened, and I thought that was interesting.

Beat.

Also she used to be a potter
she said she made voodoo dolls but
she was just joshing me.

Beat.

When are you going to come visit?

Beat—he's too busy.

No… I know…of course, yes…
No, forget it, maybe later.

Beat.

Maybe I should come visit you.

Beat—he's trying to get out of this.

We always have such fun when I visit you! I love staying
with you, your roommate is so lovely, the tall one, what's his
name… Do you know what he did last time, he did the funniest
thing, did I tell you this? He was—

*Beat—her son is saying that she has told him this SO MANY
times.*

Oh. Oh yes. I guess I did, didn't I.

Beat.

She's joined a…local farm. And she just got here yesterday! She just picked up a box of vegetables on her way here. I mean that's very healthy, she seems very healthy. And she just bought a folding bicycle, like a…like sort of a folding chair, but it's a bicycle.

Her son isn't as impressed as she is.

Anyway, she seems like a very healthy person with a very sort of *healthy* lifestyle, and I just think this is all going to just be very healthy for me.

ROBYN wanders in. She's smoking.

SHARON coughs. She coughs pointedly.

ROBYN glances at her.

ROBYN

Oh! Sorry!

SHARON coughs and fans the air.

ROBYN

Sorry!

She goes out onto the porch and chain-smokes. Back to the phone:

SHARON
(Intense whisper.)

SHE. IS. SMOKING.

Beat.

Well I thought I was fairly clear about that when I said I was looking for a woman in her fifties.

Beat.

Are you LAUGHING at me?

Beat.

I have to go.

Beat—he's apologising but she won't be mollified.

No, no it's OK. I have to go. I know how busy you are.

She hangs up.

A beat.

ROBYN comes back in.

ROBYN

Morning.

SHARON

Good morning.

Beat.

ROBYN

Sorry about that.

SHARON

I didn't know you smoked.

ROBYN

I quit. I'm quitting. I quit.

SHARON

Oh.

ROBYN

I quit right before I moved. So.

SHARON

Oh.

ROBYN

New places stress me out.

SHARON

You weren't stressed out in the Bronx but you're stressed out in Iowa?

ROBYN

I *was* stressed out in the Bronx, which is why I smoked there. And I am stressed out in Iowa, which is why I just smoked here. Even though I quit.
I am re-quitting.

SHARON

They have nicotine gum at the gas station.
They didn't used to, but now it's become popular.

ROBYN

The gum is no good, I get hooked on the gum.
I just need to quit cold turkey.
Everything that I do, I just need to DO it, no half-measures.
Just jump.

SHARON

(Impressed despite herself.)

Like moving to Iowa?

ROBYN

Like moving to Iowa.

A warmer beat between the women: a shared humour.

SHARON

Do you want some eggs? I was gonna make eggs.

ROBYN

I can't, but thanks.

SHARON

You—?
Oh!
Vegan!

ROBYN

Vegan.

SHARON

Vegan.
Coffee? Without milk?

ROBYN

I'd love some coffee. With almond milk.

SHARON

I don't have almond milk.

ROBYN

I got it from the co-op yesterday.
You can try it.

> *She gets out the almond milk.*
> *SHARON thinks it's very strange, but:*

SHARON
(Very determined.)

OK yes.
Yes, I will.

> *She lets* ROBYN *put almond milk in her coffee. They drink coffee together.*

SHARON

It's…

ROBYN

Weird?

SHARON

Weird.

ROBYN

Bad?

SHARON

Not bad.

> *Beat.*

> *The warmth between them becomes awkward again.*

SHARON

So what do you *do*?

ROBYN

Me?

SHARON

Uh. You.

ROBYN

Well. I do a lot of things.

> *SHARON waits. ROBYN drinks more almond milk coffee.*

SHARON

Oh.
Well.
Like what do you do?
For example.

ROBYN

Well.

> *Beat.*

I'm a poet.

SHARON

A poet!

ROBYN

Yes, I write poetry.

> *Beat.*

SHARON

That's great!
I love poetry!

> *Beat—honest.*

I don't really understand poetry.

ROBYN

I write slam poetry.

SHARON

I don't know what that is.

ROBYN

I write poems and then I perform them.

SHARON

And what do you write…about?

A pause.

ROBYN
I do other things too.

SHARON
Oh?

ROBYN
I grow things. I like to grow things.

SHARON
I never had much of a green thumb but
that's wonderful!
What do you grow?

A pause.

ROBYN
What do you do?

SHARON
(Completely off-balanced.)
Me?
I mean.
I live here. Obviously.

ROBYN
Yeah…

SHARON
I'm a mother…

ROBYN
Right.

SHARON
I'm retired!

ROBYN
From what?

Beat.

SHARON

My marriage.

ROBYN

Oh.

SHARON

Yeah. So.

ROBYN

I'm sorry?

SHARON

Don't be.

ROBYN

Then I'm not.

    Beat, ROBYN smiles, then SHARON does.
    A shared moment.

SHARON

I'd love to hear some of your poems.

ROBYN

Oh. I don't think so.

SHARON

Maybe you could explain them to me.

ROBYN

Poetry can't really...be explained.

SHARON

That's probably why I don't like it.
Oh! Sorry! I didn't mean...

ROBYN

No. No no. It's OK.
I don't like poetry either.

SHARON

You don't?

ROBYN

I like mine. But I don't have a lot of patience for other people's.

SHARON

I think I feel that way about children.

ROBYN

I think I feel that way about most things.

Another shared smile. Beat.

SHARON

So…why Iowa?

ROBYN

Why not Iowa?

SHARON

Do you know anybody here?

ROBYN

You.

SHARON

Me?

ROBYN

You now.
Now I know you.

This pleases SHARON.

SHARON

Well
what would you like to *do*
here?
There's the University, there's adult classes
(there's poetry!)
or
hot yoga
on North Clinton
Which I've never taken but I see everybody through the window
when I go by, and they all look so
Healthy and happy, you sort of want to injure them

but yeah, so, there's yoga…
My son thinks Iowa City is boring but
if he just visited me more often he'd see that
now it's very cultural here, Iowa City is actually very [cultural]
I mean *I* sort of haven't [been involved]
but *you* might want to [be involved]

ROBYN

I thought maybe I'd raise bees.

SHARON

Bees.

ROBYN

And maybe a sheep or
a cow or
something.

SHARON

A…sheep.

ROBYN

I don't know, I imagined
wide open skies, I think and
rising at dawn…
A sort of…restorative manual labour…

SHARON

Oh…hmm…
We could have a garden…?

ROBYN

My grandmother was from Iowa.

SHARON

She was?

ROBYN has surprised them both with this revelation. A moment.

ROBYN

I didn't know her.
But.
I heard she was from Iowa.

SHARON
(Beat—a little wistfully.)
I guess everybody wants to start over. Just burn it all down and
start over.

ROBYN
(A genuine question.)
Do you?

SHARON
I don't know…

ROBYN
You said 'everybody'. So…don't you?

SHARON
I guess I do. Sometimes.

ROBYN
Maybe you already did. When you…retired…from your marriage.

SHARON
No, that didn't feel like a…glorious blaze. It just feels—
felt
very sad. And cold.
And then there was nobody to talk to in the mornings.

   Beat.

He retired before I did.
Actually.
From the marriage.
But he didn't tell me that, so I had to find it out myself.

ROBYN
Another woman?

SHARON
No
He just started spending all his money on models of things
airplanes, trains, cars
and he'd spend all his time with those mini things
instead of with me, in our normal-sized life.

Beat.

Ha!
Maybe I'll write a…'slam' poem about that
and you can perform it.

Beat.

ROBYN

I've retired from slam poetry.
But you should do it anyway.

SHARON

I've never written a slam poem before.

Beat.

If you're no longer a poet
or a potter
what *are* you?

A beat.

ROBYN gets up.

ROBYN

It'll probably be bad, all first poems are bad poems.
There's a great liberty in being bad.

She leaves the kitchen.

SHARON stares after her, struck to the heart by this wisdom.

3.

Night. A week later.

ROBYN at the kitchen table, alone.
Her pot plants are set on the windowsill.
Very carefully, with immense precision, she rolls a joint.

SHARON comes in, phone in hand.

ROBYN

Hey!

SHARON
(Startled.)

Oh!

> *Sees.*

I thought you quit.

ROBYN

It's not tobacco.

SHARON
(Not kidding.)

Then what is it?

> *A beat. ROBYN looks at her like: SERIOUSLY?*

> *A beat. SHARON gets it.*

OH.
You—?
Are those—?
Are those drugs?

ROBYN

Sharon.

SHARON

What!

ROBYN

It's medicinal.
Medicinal herbs.

SHARON

I thought it was drugs?

ROBYN

Herbs only become drugs when a capitalist economy gets involved.

SHARON

Oh.

A beat. She sits at the kitchen table.
She can't help her curiosity.

Is there some—place—here? Where you go? And buy...herbs?

ROBYN

You mean like a long sticky alley, and a guy with a ski mask is waiting at the end of it?

SHARON

Is that...?
Is that—!

ROBYN

No!
I grew these.

Gestures to the plants.

I grow my own medicinal herbs, Sharon.

SHARON

Those are...?

ROBYN

I thought you knew. You said you liked them!

SHARON

I did like them! I thought they were just...weird...plants.

ROBYN

Oh man, Okay. Well.

Finishes rolling the joint.

Outside. Right?

SHARON

Right.

ROBYN

Right.

> *She gets up.*
> *But SHARON isn't ready to be left alone.*

SHARON

I can't get ahold of my son.

ROBYN

You called him?

SHARON

I've called. I've been calling.

ROBYN

It's a Friday night.

SHARON

I know.

ROBYN

So he's probably out.

SHARON

I texted him too.

ROBYN

Is something the matter?

SHARON

What do you mean?

ROBYN

Well if it's a Friday night and you're texting him and you're calling him, is something the matter?

> *A beat.*

SHARON

I just think it's a good thing for us to stay in touch.
For a mother and a son to stay in touch.

Don't you?

ROBYN

Yeah. Yes. I do.
But it might be better to stay in touch on a Thursday. Or in the morning.
You know?

A beat.

SHARON
      (Completely unconvinced and kind of upset.)
No, sure, of course.

A beat.

ROBYN sits back down.

ROBYN

Is he dating someone?

SHARON

Yeah.
I think so?
He doesn't really
communicate
about that kind of thing.

ROBYN

Maybe he's out with his boyfriend.

SHARON

Girlfriend.

ROBYN

Right, sorry. Straight. You said that.

SHARON

Just because he's a designer doesn't mean

ROBYN

You're right, I forgot.
Maybe he's out with his girlfriend, at a nice dinner.

SHARON

I met her once.

ROBYN

That's nice.

SHARON

She's a lesbian.

ROBYN

... Oh?

SHARON

Not that there's anything wrong with that!!

ROBYN

How long have they been dating?

SHARON

A few years.
She's got that short hair.
You know.
We went to brunch and she mentioned an ex-girlfriend.
Apparently they're friends with her ex-girlfriend.
It's all very confusing.

   A beat.

ROBYN

I was married to a man.

SHARON

You were??

ROBYN

Yeah.

SHARON

I didn't know that.

ROBYN

I've only been here a week, why would you know that?

SHARON

But then you realised you were gay? And you left him?

ROBYN

No, we were in love. And it ended badly. But we loved each other.

SHARON

(Amazed and a little scared.)

Are you…a bisexual?

ROBYN

No. I'm just saying
people find specific words for themselves because it's easier than not having words.
You know?
But
it doesn't mean those words are *all* accurate
all the time.
So if she's been with your son for years, she probably loves him.
Which means, your son probably has lots of people who love him.
Which is a good thing.
He's probably out right now with people who love him.
And if you call him in the morning, maybe he'll tell you about it.

A beat.

SHARON gets up. She goes to the cupboard, gets out some Johnny Walker.

ROBYN

Ohhh-kay.

SHARON

You want some?

ROBYN

I'm OK.

SHARON

Just a little nightcap.

ROBYN

I'm sober. But you go ahead.

SHARON
(Factually, not mean.)

You do drugs.

ROBYN

I medicate myself with medicinal herbs.
But my days with alcohol are over.

> SHARON *sits down but doesn't pour herself a drink. She studies the joint carefully.* ROBYN *gets up.*

I'm gonna have a smoke on your porch and then call it a—

SHARON
(Doesn't want to be left alone.)

I've never.
Smoked that.

ROBYN

... No?

SHARON

No.
Not even in college.
I kissed a—
I told you that.
But drugs? I never.

ROBYN

Please stop calling it that.

SHARON

Sorry.

> *Beat.*

ROBYN

Would you like some?

SHARON

Yes.
Yes please.

ROBYN

Okay.

> *She hesitates, then sits back down. Lights it up. Takes a long drag, then hands it to* SHARON.

SHARON

How do you…?

ROBYN

You just…like a cigarette.
Have you ever…?

SHARON

Once.

ROBYN

Once. Okay. Like that.
Just drag it in deep, and then hold your breath.

SHARON

This isn't gonna give me cancer, right?

ROBYN

Nope. No cancer.

SHARON

Okay.

> *She takes a deep drag.*
> *Lets it out, coughing a little, but.*

ROBYN

Yeah! Nice.

SHARON

I don't feel anything.

ROBYN

Give it a second.

SHARON

What am I going to feel?

ROBYN

Relaxed.

SHARON

Am I gonna hallucinate?

ROBYN

No! no. You'll just feel relaxed.

SHARON
(Getting more tense.)
I never feel relaxed. I'm not a relaxed person. What if I don't feel relaxed?

ROBYN

You will one hundred per cent feel relaxed.

SHARON takes another drag, just in case.
Then gives the joint back to ROBYN.

SHARON

I think my son doesn't like me.

ROBYN

I'm sure that's not

SHARON

He *loves* me. I know he *loves* me.
But I think he doesn't like me very much.

ROBYN

Our kids don't have to like us, they just have to survive long enough to become us.

SHARON

Do you have kids?!

Beat.

ROBYN passes the joint back to SHARON.

ROBYN

Your turn.

Beat. SHARON takes another drag.

SHARON

You didn't tell me you—

ROBYN

Sharon.

SHARON

Yeah?

A half-beat. In lieu of saying 'shut up':

ROBYN

Tell me more about your son.

Half-beat.

SHARON

He's very smart.
He's very good-looking.
I know it's strange for a mother to say that about her own—
but it's true. He's a very attractive boy.
And I don't know where he gets that from because his father
Good lord.
That man looked like a potato.

ROBYN

He probably got it from you.

SHARON

Me?
No!
Me?

Beat.

Do you think I'm good-looking?

ROBYN

I think you're pretty, yeah.

SHARON

Do you mean that in a factual way, or a lesbian way?

Half-beat.

ROBYN

I think I need you to make the distinction for me.

SHARON

Sorry. I'm sorry. I said it all wrong.
I just meant
Like, there's a way a man would say to me: you're pretty.
And that would mean I was actually pretty.
And there's a way a woman—a straight woman, I guess—
would say that to me.
And it would mean that she felt sorry for me.
And I don't really know what it means when a lesbian person
says that to me because I haven't ever really known any lesbian
people before, except for—

ROBYN

Your son's girlfriend.

SHARON

Right.

ROBYN

Right.

SHARON

And she didn't like me.
I think she thought I was boring.
And possibly judgmental but I don't think I was judgmental
I didn't feel judgmental I just felt confused.
Am I high?
Maybe I think I'm high?

ROBYN

I think you're just getting relaxed.
Okay. Well.
I said it like: factually, I think you are factually pretty.
And I don't feel sorry for you.
But I'm not hitting on you.

SHARON

Oh! Thank you.
That's very clear.

ROBYN

Good.

SHARON

But nuanced.

ROBYN

Yes.

SHARON

But now it's clear. Thank you.

ROBYN

You're welcome.

A beat. They smoke.

We should turn some music on.

SHARON

Music?

ROBYN

Yeah.
No?

SHARON

I don't really listen to music?

Beat.

I have this CD…
My son sent it to me
for Christmas one year
he couldn't come home so
in the mornings I'd make breakfast
and just play that CD.

ROBYN

Let's hear it.

SHARON

Okay.
Okay!

She presses PLAY on an old CD player nestled on a shelf. Her CD plays—a sentimental song that's SO TERRIBLE, but also, it kind of moves us, in ways we will never admit to later. (Possibly Mary Chapin Carpenter.)

They listen to the CD and get high.

SHARON

I've never
you know [smoked pot]
with anyone
I mean obviously because I've never [smoked pot]
but
this is really nice.
No wonder all the kids do drugs.
Oops.
Sorry.
Medicinal...
drugs.

ROBYN
(Laughing.)

'All the kids' don't

SHARON

Don't they?

ROBYN

Not *all*.

SHARON

Well they should.
All of them maybe should.
Also, I should've been in a band.

ROBYN

A band!

SHARON

Were you ever in a band?
I bet you were in a band.

ROBYN

Sort of, when I was in college.

SHARON

I knew it!!

ROBYN

I told this girl that I was in a band to impress her.
Then she asked me out, and I actually had to be in a band.

They're laughing together. Then:

SHARON
(Very gently.)

Where's your child?

ROBYN

What?

SHARON

Or children.

A beat. ROBYN could say anything. Then she gets up, decisively.

ROBYN

We need new music.

She gets her iPhone. She plays some kind of faster, grittier music. Maybe Patti Smith's 'Dancing Barefoot'.

SHARON

… What is that?

ROBYN

New music.

She starts to dance.
A beat. SHARON gets up too. She dances.
Both women dance in the kitchen, by themselves, but together.

JEN SILVERMAN

4.

Next day. Kitchen.

ROBYN, on the landline.
She looks over her shoulder.
She doesn't want to be overheard.
She takes a deep breath.

ROBYN

Hello!
Yes, uh
yes I'm calling for Amanda.
Well
when will she be back?
Oh.
Well.
Did she give you any sort of
ballpark idea of—
No no
that's OK
I'll just
I'll try again.

> *She hangs up. A beat.*
> *A deep breath. Resolve!*

> *She picks up the phone again. Dials.*

Hi. Yes. I'm calling back.
Yes, for Amanda.
Yes I know you said that
but we both know she told you to say that
and right now she's there
standing behind you
and you're darting her kind of wide-eyed looks
like WHAT DO I DO ABOUT THIS
and she's shaking her head
and biting her fingernails
so you know what
I *do* want to leave a message.

You tell my daughter that I'm doing it.
She thinks I can't do it but I'm doing it.
I'm in *Iowa*
of all places
so.
That's all.
I'm going to hang up now.

> *ROBYN hangs up.*
> *A beat. Another deep breath.*
> *She goes out on the porch.*

> *SHARON enters the kitchen.*
> *She doesn't see ROBYN at first.*
> *She calls her son.*
> *It goes to voicemail.*

SHARON

Hiii
it's me
your mother
um
it's Saturday morning
I just wanted to make sure you got home OK
from wherever you were
whatever you were doing
with whoever it was

> *Beat.*

Also are you still dating that lesbian girl?

> *Beat.*

It's OK if you are

> *Beat.*

You should visit me!

> *Beat.*

Also, I just have been thinking

maybe you don't tell me enough things
about your life
and
maybe you don't want to tell me
(which I guess is OK)
(although I don't know why you wouldn't)
but I *do* want to know.
Because
I care.
So.

>   *Beat—this comes bursting out of her.*

I smoked marijuana last night.

>   *A frozen moment, she's shocked at herself.*

Goodbye.

>   *She hangs up. A beat.*

>   *ROBYN comes in from the porch.*

SHARON
(Startled.)

Oh!

ROBYN

Just me, again.

SHARON

Good morning.

ROBYN

Morning.

SHARON

How'd you sleep?

ROBYN

Good. You?

SHARON
(Finds this to be true, as she says it.)

Really good.

A warm beat between them.

Coffee?

ROBYN

I'd love some.

SHARON

Okay!

The phone rings. They both freeze. Then both move to it.

ROBYN

It's / for me.

SHARON
(Same time.)

Oh god.

Beat—ROBYN is quizzical:

I mean, go on.

ROBYN
(Answers the phone.)

Hello?

It's SHARON's son.

Oh!
Uh. Hello. Hi.
Oh, this is Robyn, your mother's roommate.
Yeah, nice to meet you as well.
Yeah, your mom is—

On sudden whim, SHARON starts shaking her head frantically.
ROBYN pauses, startled.
Head-shaking continues.

Your mom is not
available
right now.

Beat.

Yeah she's busy.

Beat.

No, I don't know what she's doing, I just know she's…

SHARON gestures emphatically: OUT.

OUT. She. is OUT. right now.
What?
Well I guess she must've stepped out right after she called you.

Beat—he's asking her something.

Marijuana?
Your mother?
I have no idea.
You'll have to ask her that.
Okay.
Okay.
You too.

ROBYN hangs up.

A beat. Co-conspirators. Then:

ROBYN

You told him you smoked pot?

SHARON

I didn't mean to
I meant to say something else
some bullshit Mom thing
stay safe, be careful, don't ride the subway at night
and then I said that. Instead.

Beat.

ROBYN

He sounds nice.

SHARON

He does?

ROBYN

Yeah.
He had a nice voice.

    Beat.

SHARON

I'm always home in the mornings.
He's going to ask where I was.

ROBYN
(Shrugs.)

You were out.

SHARON

I don't really *go* out.

ROBYN
(Teasing her.)

But I hear there's poetry classes and
hot yoga and

SHARON

—okay okay—

ROBYN

cultural [things]

SHARON

I go to the book club.
And the store. On Thursdays.

ROBYN

The store?

SHARON

I work at a gift shop. Just on Thursdays. It's nice.
Maybe I'll say I went in today as well. Early.

ROBYN

Tell him you were on a date.

SHARON

What?

ROBYN

Yeah. A date.

SHARON

Noooo
A—!
On a *Saturday morning*?

ROBYN

Breakfast date.

SHARON

Oh man.

ROBYN

You met him online. He asked you to breakfast. What.

SHARON

Online?

ROBYN

Don't tell me you never…

   She sees SHARON hasn't.

You *never*?

SHARON

There are *serial killers* online.

ROBYN

Oh my god.
Time out. Time.
You have *never* been on an internet date.

SHARON

No!! Have you??

ROBYN

 Yes!

SHARON

Oh!

   Beat.

There aren't any women serial killers though. So that's different.

ROBYN

When was the last time you were on a date?

SHARON

When I got married! And we all saw how well *that* turned out!

ROBYN

Okay.
Okay.
We have to remedy this.

SHARON

No we don't. Nope.

ROBYN

Sharon. You have to stop thinking about yourself as basically dead.
You are actually younger than most US presidents.
You are young enough that, if you were a president, you would be a *young* president.
OK?
So just. Stop mummifying yourself.

> *A beat. This strikes* SHARON *all the way to the heart. After a moment:*

SHARON

I'd go on a date if you went.

ROBYN

What! Oh no no no

SHARON

Like a double

ROBYN

I am not going on your date with you!

SHARON

Like a double date, what

ROBYN

Awkward! That shit was awkward in college, it's awkward now!

SHARON

Someone with a sister

ROBYN

No! No no

SHARON

We could all get coffee together

ROBYN

No! I will help screen the applicants so that you do not find yourself sitting across from a serial killer, but I'm not gonna come along and have coffee with his sister!

SHARON

You'd help me screen them?

ROBYN

Yeah I could do that.

SHARON

I don't know how to set up a...page. A home page.

ROBYN

A profile.
I could help you do that.

SHARON

How come you know all these things?

A beat.

ROBYN

I used to run a lot of businesses.

SHARON

You did?

ROBYN

Yeah.

SHARON

What kind of businesses?

ROBYN

Businesses that helped people with personal things.

SHARON

I didn't know that.

ROBYN

We're just getting to know each other. There's a lot you don't know.

SHARON

(Doesn't mean to say this.)
I'm glad you're here, Robyn.

ROBYN is moved, and this makes her awkward. A beat. Then:

ROBYN

I'll just...
I forgot my glasses.

She leaves the room.

A beat. Sharon dRINKS coffee.

The phone rings. Sharon CONSIDErs.
She considers. She sighs.
Sharon pICKS It up.

SHARON

Hi.

Beat. It's not her son.

Excuse me?
No, this is Sharon. Who's calling please?
Amanda, I think you have the wrong number.
No, there isn't anyone here by that name.
Victoria, there's no Victoria—
What?
No, I'm not...
I just said, there's no Victoria here.
You have the wrong number, dear.
What do you mean she just called you from—

A beat.

I don't know what to tell you.
I have to go.

> *SHARON hangs up.*
> *She sits for a second.*
> *She opens her mouth.*
> *She closes it.*

> *A beat.*

> *ROBYN returns.*

ROBYN

Did I hear the phone?

SHARON

It was
just
my son.
Calling back.

ROBYN

You picked up?

SHARON

I told him
I couldn't talk.
I was going on a date.

5.

Later that morning.

The porch. ROBYN's boxes still stacked.
SHARON goes through her things.
She doesn't know exactly what she's looking for, but she knows there's something.

SHARON
(Reading the box labels.)

Kitchen supplies
Odds and ends
books
okay
cook books
really?
you don't cook
I've never seen you
winter clothes
okay
Antiques
I like antiques
clothes

> *She opens the clothing box.*
> *Looks at ROBYN's clothes. Takes them out.*

> *Beat.*

> *Puts on a hat.*

> *Beat.*

> *Puts on a jacket.*
> *Models.*

> *She tries on ROBYN's clothes. She feels powerful in them.*
> *She moves around the porch in them.*
> *Clears her throat. Sort of as ROBYN:*

I'm a poet.
I write poems.
Here's a poem.

*Silently pretends to recite The Best Poem That Has Ever
Been Written.*

Thank you.
Thank you.
An autograph?
Oh my.
I suppose I could.

> *SHARON keeps going through the clothing box.
> Then: she double-takes.*

Oh.

> *She reaches in. She pulls out a fistful of driving licences. Beat.
> Another fistful. She reads the names, dropping them back
> into the box.*

Claire Jones.
Claire Doyle.
Sarah Lucas.
Victoria Lucas.
Robyn Doyle.
Victoria Jones.

> *Beat, more fistfuls of driving licences, she drops them back
> without reading them, beat.*

Oh.

6.

Evening.

SHARON sits at the kitchen table.
She waits for ROBYN to get home.
Key in the lock.
ROBYN enters.

ROBYN

Oh!
Hey!

SHARON

Hi.

ROBYN

How was your day?

SHARON

Good
how was yours?

ROBYN

I went to the Farmer's Market on
what is that street
the one with the parking garage

SHARON

Gilbert

ROBYN

Yeah, Gilbert! I bought a necklace
there was this woman selling these necklaces she'd made
out of hemp I think, she grew it herself, and these clay beads,
do you know who I'm talking about? Is she maybe in your book
club or something?

SHARON

How come you have so many driving licences?

    A real beat.

ROBYN

Excuse me?

SHARON

I asked how come—?

ROBYN

Did you go through my stuff??

SHARON

I was looking for
a hat

ROBYN

A *hat*?

SHARON

My head was
cold.

ROBYN

A *hat* in my *stuff*?

SHARON

It said 'clothes'.
I thought, maybe Robyn has a hat.

ROBYN

Okay.
Wow.

SHARON

I'm sorry.
I don't mean it like…
you *shouldn't* have a hundred driving licences
but also
why do you have them?

ROBYN

Because.
Because I do. I collect them.

SHARON

They're all you, but with different names.

ROBYN

Right.

SHARON

And different addresses and different birthdays.

ROBYN

I mean did you examine every single one?

SHARON

Who's Amanda?

A real beat.

ROBYN

Did she call?

SHARON

Yeah.
She asked for Victoria.
Who is she?

ROBYN

Is this 20 questions? Are we doing the roommate get-to-know-you thing, or is this 20 questions, or is this an interrogation?

SHARON

I'm not interrogating—

ROBYN

Do you want me to leave?

SHARON

I'm not asking you to leave!

Beat.

Should I be asking you to leave?

Beat.

ROBYN

No.

Beat.

SHARON

Then I'm not.

Beat.

Are you hungry?

ROBYN

Am I...?

SHARON

No dairy. No meat. I made vegetables.

ROBYN

What did you make?

SHARON

I just kind of cut them up and cooked them. I don't know. You don't have to...

ROBYN

I'll try some.

Beat. SHARON gets her a bowl of vegetables.

They sit. Eventually:

ROBYN

Have you talked to anyone about this?

SHARON

'This'?

ROBYN

This
me
this

                    SHARON

No!
Who would I—?
No

                    ROBYN

Okay.

                    SHARON

What should I not be telling people?

                    ROBYN

Nothing. There's nothing to not-tell.
I came here for some peace and quiet.

                    SHARON

Look, I'm not trying to
I don't mean to
I *like* you

        This surprises them both, greatly.

        A beat.

What I mean is
it's nice
to have a friend.

                    ROBYN

Are we friends?

                    SHARON

Aren't we?

                    ROBYN

I thought we were roommates.
House, housemates

                    SHARON

We are.
But
then you got me high so
now we're friends.

A beat. Amused despite herself:

ROBYN

Is that how it works?

SHARON

That's how it seems to work when the kids do it.

ROBYN
(Laughs, then sobers.)

All right
if we're *friends*
don't go through my shit.

SHARON

I didn't mean to

ROBYN

Yeah I know you wanted a hat
if you want a hat, buy a damn hat

SHARON

Okay

    Beat.

Is Amanda your daughter?

ROBYN

Jesus Christ.

SHARON

I'm very nosy and I'm very persistent
it's something that has always irritated my son
but inescapable, in our line of work

ROBYN
(Alarmed.)

Line of work!

SHARON

Being a mother.

    Beat.

ROBYN

Yes.

SHARON

Yes?

ROBYN

Yes.
You are correct.
Amanda is my daughter.
Yes.

SHARON

Oh.

    Beat.

What's your name actually?

ROBYN

Robyn.

SHARON

But... Victoria? And Clare? And...?

ROBYN

Those were also my names, actually, when they were actually
my names.

SHARON

But what were you born as?

ROBYN

I was born as a malleable, changeable template.

    Beat.

SHARON

Is that a poem?

ROBYN

No.

    Beat.

SHARON

I guess what I'm asking is,
Are you doing something illegal?

ROBYN

Right now?

SHARON

Or like…recently.
Or…ongoingly.
Or like…were you?

A beat.

ROBYN

Yes.
Yes I *was*, Sharon.

SHARON

Oh!

A beat.

What was it?

ROBYN

If you ask me that
and I tell you
it makes you an accomplice
so.

Beat.

SHARON
(Trying the word out.)

An accomplice.

Beat.

What did you do?

ROBYN

Sharon.

SHARON

Yeah?

ROBYN

I'm going to go outside and have a cigarette.
And you think about whether or not you want me to answer that.
And when I come back, you can ask it again.
Or
we can finish dinner
and make an online dating profile for you,
and go to bed
and tomorrow will be a whole new day
in which this question does not exist.

She gets up and starts to leave to the porch.

SHARON

Are you really gonna quit smoking, or is that like
part of this whole
multiple personality thing?

ROBYN

I, as me, as myself, am *going* to quit
as soon as I have this next, last,
cigarette.

ROBYN goes outside.

A beat.

SHARON wants to do so many things!
She gets up
she sits down
she gets up
she opens her mouth
she sits down
she goes to the phone
checking nervously over her shoulder.

ROBYN isn't looking.
She calls her son.

Voicemail!

She has no idea what she's going to say.
She sort of listens to herself stumble through the usual set of communications, while wondering if she's going to tell him what's happening.

SHARON

Hi
it's me
your mother
um
I just wanted to see how you're doing!
I just
am thinking about you and
I think you should visit.
I think we should visit each other.
When I told you I smoked marijuana?
I was kidding.
…
I went on a date.
Actually, I wasn't kidding.
I did smoke marijuana.
But I'm not smoking it right now.
…
I didn't go on a date.
I *did* go on a date.
…
My roommate is very
she's very
there's something very
about her
the thing is
…
she's an interesting person.

> *SHARON is so surprised!*
> *She didn't expect to say this!*
> *But it's true.*

She knows things.
She does things.
Everybody always told me not to do things.
Your father never [understood me]
And my mother! She always said *Don't*.
Is that how you feel about me?
Am I a person who says to you: *Don't*?

Beat—maybe she doesn't want that answered.

Robyn just says: Do. And then she *does*.

The voicemail cuts her off.

Are you there?
Are you...?
Oh.

She calls back, voicemail.

Your machine cut me off.
I won't keep you too long.
I just wanted to say that
I'm very
happy
and
that's all.
Goodbye.

She hangs up.

ROBYN enters from the porch.
A beat between them.

ROBYN

I finished my cigarette.

SHARON
(With real resolve.)
What do you do, Robyn?

ROBYN

Did.

SHARON

What *did* you do?

A beat. Okay.

ROBYN

I took people's money.

SHARON

Like. You robbed them?

ROBYN

Yes.

SHARON

You mugged them?

ROBYN

No. I convinced them to give me their money.

SHARON

That doesn't sound illegal.

ROBYN

Under false pretenses.
I called them up. Old people. Mostly.
They could donate to save the whales or the orphans or the
ozone layer. Whatever.
And they did.
And it all went to me.

SHARON
(Horrified...but also impressed.)
You did that?

ROBYN

Yeah.
But that wasn't enough money.
So then I started telling people they'd won things.
People are a lot more willing to risk when there's tangible reward.
And to collect the prize, they'd have to provide information.

SHARON

Are you the Nigerians?

ROBYN

Sorry?

SHARON

All those emails from Princess whatsit trying to store her millions in my whatever—were those actually from *you*?

ROBYN

Oh! No. I'm much more detail-oriented.

SHARON

But that's the general idea.

ROBYN

That's the general idea, yes.

    A beat as SHARON takes this all in.

Do you want me to stop telling you?

SHARON

No,
go on.

ROBYN

… So that happened for a while.
And it was actually substantially lucrative.

SHARON

What about your daughter??
Did she know?

ROBYN

We teach our children whatever skill sets we have, Sharon.
Didn't you?

SHARON

You *taught* your *daughter* how to *scam* people?

ROBYN

She's the one who came up with the driving licence thing.

We started manufacturing fake IDs, and then she'd sell them at school.
But that wasn't until college.

SHARON

Your *daughter* is a *con-artist*?

ROBYN

My daughter is an intelligent and resourceful young woman.

A beat.

SHARON

I don't know.

ROBYN

What.

SHARON

What you said…before.
I don't know if I gave my son any kind of…
skill set.

ROBYN

He sounds successful.

SHARON

I think he might have done that on his own.
Or, worse, in spite of me.
We're not close.

ROBYN

Well. Amanda and I aren't close either.

SHARON

You *scammed* people together.
You were *con-artists* together.
You were like Bonnie and Clyde, but mother and daughter.
That's so… I don't know! Close!

ROBYN

We have to give our kids things, and they have to reject those things.

At some point.
Amanda temps at a law firm now and she wears these little power suits
and she tells everybody that her mother lives in another country
so all of her boyfriends bring her home for the holidays
and their mothers are extra sympathetic because her own is so far away.
So.

A beat.

SHARON

I'm sorry.

ROBYN

It's fine.

SHARON

It's not fine.

Beat.

ROBYN

She doesn't think I can give it up. The lifestyle.
But I mean, I'm in *Iowa*. Talk about giving up.

SHARON

(Hey)

ROBYN

Also, I sold pot. But you probably figured that out already.

SHARON
(Wide-eyed.)

No, I didn't.

ROBYN

You didn't?

SHARON

No! How would I figure that out??

ROBYN
(Genuinely impressed.)
Wow. What planet are you from?

SHARON
Iowa?

ROBYN
Wow. Iowa.

SHARON
Actually Illinois, though.

ROBYN
Right. I remember.

SHARON
Not quite the Land of Giving Up.

ROBYN
I was
talking about me, not you
maybe also you, but mostly me.

SHARON
You sold pot?

ROBYN
Not too often. Just because I don't really have a growhouse or
anything.
And growing pot for real, that's a commitment, it requires a lot
of specifics.
But I have definitely sold it. And that has also, sporadically,
definitely been lucrative.

SHARON
Did Amanda sell pot?

ROBYN
(With some pride.)
She paid her way through college.

SHARON

Wow.

ROBYN
(Really proud.)
And she has a green thumb, I mean I'm not bad with plants but she's got a real talent.

SHARON
(Impressed.)
That's great.

ROBYN

It was.

   Beat.

She refuses to talk about any of that now.
When we talk, which is not often, she wants to keep things 'present tense'.
She says her therapist told her to do that.
And I'm like, what kind of a therapist refuses to speak in the past tense?
Things *happened*. They *accumulated*. We *became*.
Or the future, for that matter. *We will become.*
But no. Amanda says, 'Today I am eating a sandwich. I am grocery shopping.'
She says, 'We are avoiding conflict.'

   Half-beat.

I don't think conflict is a bad thing.

SHARON
You know my son does that too
the present tense thing
I don't know if anybody told him to do it
But I'll be like, 'Remember when I visited you and we had fun?'
And he'll be like, 'It's sunny today. It's cloudy today.'

   A contemplative beat, then:

What else did you do?

ROBYN

I mean, I did just a little bit of auto theft, but

SHARON

YOU WHAT.

ROBYN
(With growing pride.)

But it's a lot of work
high risk
you have to be really really good at it
and that takes time
like a real commitment to craft

SHARON

Okay yeah I mean yeah I imagine

ROBYN

And you have to spend real time building the right networks
and people have to trust you
if you're going to buy stolen property you have to trust the seller

SHARON

Sure OK

ROBYN

And I was *good*
buyers trusted me
and you might not know this from looking at me but
I'm very very good with cars
both jacking them and stripping them down
some people don't do well under pressure and
I don't want to brag, but I would say that I sort of
thrive
in those contexts
but
finally in the end
auto theft just ended up not being time-cost effective. You know?

SHARON

Right!
… Why not?

ROBYN

… Well
because we moved a lot, we had to move a lot
so you build a network of buyers and then you abandon it,
sort of before you've closed the deal.
It becomes wasteful. And ultimately too risky.

SHARON

Are people chasing you?

ROBYN

Right now?

SHARON

Yes, right now!!

ROBYN

I don't think they are *right now*, no.

SHARON

You don't *think?*

ROBYN

I'm fairly certain that *right now* nobody is chasing me.

SHARON

How certain?

ROBYN

Fairly.

    A beat.

SHARON

Are you doing something right now? Here?

ROBYN

I just got here.

SHARON
(A real question.)
Are you scamming me?

ROBYN

You?

SHARON

Me.

ROBYN

You haven't given me any money! How am I scamming you?

SHARON

I don't know, I don't know if you are
I'm just asking.

ROBYN

Do you feel like I'm scamming you?

SHARON

I mean I don't know
Maybe my jewellry is missing or
maybe you've photocopied my credit cards or something
Have you?
I don't know
Have you?

ROBYN

No.

SHARON

No?

ROBYN

No. I have not.

SHARON

Promise?

ROBYN

I mean, I promise but
do you believe me?

Beat. SHARON looks at her. Then:

SHARON

Yeah.

ROBYN

Yeah?

SHARON

I do believe you. Yes.

Beat between them.

ROBYN

So that's me.

Beat.

Are you having a nervous breakdown?

Beat.

SHARON

Show me how to do it.

ROBYN

What?

SHARON

I want to do it.
What you did.

ROBYN

No!

SHARON

Why not?

ROBYN

Because…!

SHARON

Because what?

ROBYN

Because I'm done with all that.

SHARON

I'm not asking you to do it, just to show me how.

A real beat.
ROBYN takes her in. Then:

ROBYN

Show you how what, exactly?

SHARON

The phone thing.

ROBYN

I don't do the phone thing anymore.

SHARON

I bet I'd be good, talking to somebody on the phone.

ROBYN

I don't do any of this anymore.

SHARON

Like you don't smoke anymore?

Beat.

ROBYN

That's not fair.

SHARON

I'm sorry.

ROBYN

Those are entirely different things.

SHARON

I know.
You're right, I know.
Look. All I'm saying is
how
exactly
did you do it—
when you did it
(which you no longer do)?

Beat.

ROBYN

Well.
There's a few ways.
Either you're asking them for something
or you're telling them something.

SHARON

Okay...

ROBYN

Like, maybe you're telling them that something they value is about to expire.
Auto insurance. Home insurance. Their cable. Whatever.
And you have a deal, and it's kind of an amazing one-time deal, but it's ending in 24 hours. You just caught them at the tail end of this deal.

SHARON

Right.

ROBYN

So they better decide fast if they want to save 60% on their phone bill.
Or upgrade to a new twice-as-fast high-speed internet connection.

SHARON

That sounds easy. I could do that.

ROBYN

But you also have to be personable, keep them on the line until you get their credit card.
It's easy to hang up a phone.

SHARON

I'm personable.

ROBYN

It's harder than you think.

SHARON

It doesn't sound that hard.

ROBYN

Oh really!
Ring ring. I'm gonna pick up.

She 'picks up'.

Hello?

SHARON

Wait, are we pretending?

ROBYN

(We're seeing how good you are)
Hello, who is this?

SHARON

This is Sharon.

ROBYN

I don't know any Sharons.

SHARON

My name is Sharon, and I'm calling about your...
uh
your
life insurance.
Which is about to expire.

ROBYN

It is?

SHARON
(Helpfully.)
You are about to expire.

ROBYN

Let's start with something easier.
You're calling me about my cable bill. Isn't it high? Wouldn't I
like it to be lower?

SHARON

Isn't it high?

ROBYN

I guess it is a little…

SHARON

Wouldn't you like it to be lower?

ROBYN

Are you trying to sell me something?
(They get suspicious)
Are you trying to sell me something I don't want, Sharon?

SHARON

I'm calling because
there's a deal and it's about to end
and you're lucky, you are a lucky person
because first of all, there aren't that many deals in life
life is mostly about being charged the full amount
and second of all, timing is everything.
A bullet is a bullet and your head is your head and
if two seconds separate those things
well
those two seconds saved your life.
So.
How would you like to pay less for your cable?

> *A beat.* ROBYN *is actually impressed.*

ROBYN

I'd like that a lot.

SHARON

Okay!
Well that's good.
I'd like that too.
Give me your credit card.

ROBYN

(Make that sound more official. Anything about money has to
sound official, so they feel safe.)

SHARON

Please give me your credit card.

JEN SILVERMAN

ROBYN

(Breaks the 'call'.)

'The next step requires your date of birth and your credit card information.'

You don't need it, it *is required.*

SHARON

You *are* good at this.

ROBYN

Yeah, I am, I'm very good at it.

SHARON

How did I do?

ROBYN

Generally? You did OK generally

SHARON

Okay?

ROBYN

You did pretty OK.

SHARON

I was good.
You know I was good.

ROBYN

You were pretty good.

SHARON

I was personable. And you liked me.

Half-beat.

ROBYN

Yeah.
Yes. You were.

SHARON

You did, didn't you.

ROBYN

Yeah, I liked you.

A moment between them.

The air has shifted suddenly, and they both suddenly feel it, and neither is sure what the shift is. They're both suddenly uneasy.

ROBYN

So. That was that.

SHARON

I want to do it for real.

ROBYN

Sharon…

SHARON

I could do it for real, couldn't I.

A beat.

ROBYN

I…can't.
Not anymore.

SHARON

You can't? Or you don't want to?
Or you want to, but you think you shouldn't?

A beat.

ROBYN

I'm going to bed.
So.

SHARON

Look.
Tomorrow I make one phone call.
OK? Just one. With you.
And if it doesn't go well, then forget it!
I wasn't cut out for it! We'll forget it!
It'll be like it never happened.

But if it goes well
then
you see how you feel about that.

    A beat.

ROBYN

Sharon…

SHARON

One foot in the grave, who would I even tell.

ROBYN

Sharon, I told you, you are *not old.*

SHARON

I didn't feel old. Just now.
I felt like
I was *thriving*
and I bet you did too.

    A beat.

ROBYN

Good night.

    She leaves.

7.

Morning. The kitchen.

Coffee. Light. French.
… French?
Yes, SHARON is listening to a French language tape as she makes
coffee.

FRENCH TAPE

Répétez s'il vous plaît.
Je m'appelle…

SHARON

Je m'appelle Sharon.

FRENCH TAPE

Comment-allez vous?

SHARON

Comment-allez vous?

FRENCH TAPE

J'aime Paris.

SHARON

J'aime Paris.

ROBYN in the doorway.

ROBYN

What are you doing.

SHARON
(Shuts the tape off.)
Parlez-vous Français?

ROBYN

Not to any functional degree, non.
Why are you parlez-ing Français?

SHARON

I always wanted to learn.

ROBYN

You did?

SHARON

In college I was a member of the French club.

ROBYN

I didn't know that.

SHARON

I was going to be a spy. *La Femme Sharon.*
Or a baker.
… Coffee?

ROBYN

Yes please.

    SHARON gets her coffee.

SHARON

So…

ROBYN

Yeah?

SHARON

Have you
you know.
thought about it?

ROBYN

'It'…

SHARON

You know…

ROBYN

I *just* woke up.

SHARON

I know, I made you coffee.

ROBYN

So give it a minute, OK?

SHARON

Okay.

She sits and watches ROBYN drink her coffee.
With baleful focus.
Like an iguana.

ROBYN

Do you mind.

SHARON

What.

ROBYN

You're *watching* me.

SHARON

I'm drinking my coffee.

ROBYN

You are *not* drinking your coffee
you are *watching* me.

SHARON lifts her coffee cup to her mouth.
She gives ROBYN an iguana stare over the lip of the mug.

Did you sleep?

SHARON

Yeah I slept

ROBYN

Because I heard
French
around five am...?

SHARON

How did you know who to target?

ROBYN

'Target' I don't use that word 'target'

SHARON

OK...

ROBYN

'Identify', I took some time to identify my client base

SHARON

OK...
So like...

ROBYN

Northerners are mean and paranoid
Southerners are nice but suspicious
The West Coast is in a state of anarchy

SHARON

And Iowa?

ROBYN

The Midwest is always good.

  Beat.

SHARON

We could call Tanya.

ROBYN

Tanya.

SHARON

She's from Idaho.

ROBYN

Your friend Tanya?

SHARON

She's an acquaintance.

ROBYN

You want to target Tanya.

SHARON

I am identifying our best client base.

  ROBYN really takes SHARON in. Really in.

ROBYN

You're a quick study.

SHARON
(This compliment means a lot to her.)
My mother always said I was slow.

ROBYN
(Not meanly.)
Your mother was a bitch, I think.

SHARON
(Startled, not upset.)
Excuse me?

ROBYN
(Still not mean.)
I mean it's hard to tell, it was an earlier time,
sometimes you think: *that's just how women were taught to be*
but it sounds like your mother was kind of a bitch.

SHARON
I don't feel comfortable saying that myself but I really
appreciate that you said it.

A beat.

ROBYN
You'd have to disguise your voice.
An accent of some kind.

SHARON
I think I could do French.

ROBYN
Convincingly?

SHARON
Tanya is from *Idaho.*

ROBYN
If this goes badly, I never agreed to it.

SHARON
Understood.

She goes to the phone. She dials Tanya.

ROBYN sits, arms folded, a commanding general surveying the troops. SHARON blossoms under her undivided attention. In the following sequence, we see SHARON come fully alive. In a French accent.

SHARON

Hello?
Yes, is this Tanya?
Tanya, hello, this is
Juliette
Du Bois
from the Franco-Global Society of International Orphans
based in Normandy, France
Yes
Normandy is a lovely city
there are stone walls and it is right next to the ocean
and long ago people stormed the beaches with great passion

ROBYN clears her throat.

which is all to say
I wonder if you are interested in saving the lives of starving
children
orphans, *oui*, orphans
in Senegal
in many places, but specifically Senegal
have you been?
it's lovely
the bright colors, the drums, the hats
yes, Senegal is a place of music and motion and hats
and children without parents
—What?
well
what we do is, we provide orphans with things they generally lack
like *pain au chocolat*
and bicycles
and vegetables
and small hats
and the right kinds of love.
And love requires money.

All kinds of love, but especially the right kinds.
There can be no love of any kinds
without money.

> *Beat—this comes from a personal place.*

> *SHARON thinks about her life as she speaks, and she gets emotional, and it's actually weirdly honest and raw.*

Think about what it is to be alone.
It is a late night somewhere
wherever you are
and you are alone.
Think about the objects you arrange around you.
But everything is cold under your hand.
And then someone comes into your life.
And you become different.
You find yourself to be…truly…alive.
Think about how one person can change an entire lifetime
of accumulated coldness and objects and silence.

> *Beat—Tanya is affected by this and wants to help. SHARON makes direct eye contact with ROBYN, speaking with a quiet and inarguable victory:*

Merci Tanya.
It's people like you who make the difference.
The next step requires your date of birth
and your credit card information.

8.

The kitchen, two weeks later.

The table is cluttered, piled high with French guidebooks, a stack of new clothes with labels still on, scattered cash, cigarettes. AND...a record player. Stacks of credit card applications litter the table. It looks like the kitchen of high-rolling and sophisticated college kids with money to burn.

ROBYN, at the table, bagging weed.

SHARON is on the cordless phone with a book club lady. She looks younger, somehow, more buoyant.

> **SHARON**
> *(To the phone.)*
> Yes, how much would you like?
> Now, was that the herbal mix or the baked goods?
> OK dear, I'll bring it to book club tomorrow.
> Bye bye now.

> *She hangs up.*

> That's another order.

> **ROBYN**
> Boom!
> Of the brownies, or...?

> **SHARON**
> The herbal mix.

> **ROBYN**
> *(Makes a note in a notebook.)*
> Got it.
> They're being discreet?

> **SHARON**
> Like little mice
> little Iowan church mice
> but I must say, it livens up reading group discussion.
> Everybody's got opinions now,
> they all interrupt each other.

These days Tanya giggles a lot
we read that book about child soldiers and she just
giggled her way through that.

ROBYN
(Laughing.)
Was that one your pick?

SHARON
I told you—

ROBYN
You're not from here.

SHARON
I played the clarinet as a child.
Tanya refers to her book club as a—

SHARON and ROBYN
(Together.)
—reading group.

SHARON
I *seem* Iowan, but I'm *not* Iowan, it's my secret weapon.

ROBYN
Yeah I'm learning that about you.

SHARON
What?

ROBYN
Your secret weapons.

A beat between them.

SHARON
(Pleased.)
You're the one who came home yesterday with a record player.

ROBYN
You're the one who never listens to music
It was an act of mercy on my part

SHARON

I like it.
The record player.

ROBYN
(Shy.)

Yeah?

SHARON

Yeah.

ROBYN

Cool.

   Beat.

SHARON

Robyn?

ROBYN

Yeah?

SHARON

I was gonna ask you...

ROBYN

What's up?

SHARON

Well
I had this idea
this thought
that I wanted to sort of
run by you

ROBYN

Yes...?

SHARON

I just have been thinking
that
the book club ladies have been really really
receptive
to medicinal herbs

ROBYN

Sure seems like it.

SHARON

I was talking to Betty—

ROBYN

The one with the hairnet?

SHARON

Yes, and she mentioned that her god-daughter had one of our brownies

ROBYN

Oh wait a minute

SHARON

Sort of by accident but she really enjoyed it

ROBYN

How old is she?

SHARON

Twelve?

ROBYN

OH my god

SHARON

(It's fine!) and it occurred to me
you know
those kids have a whole demographic available to them that
we don't
and I thought
what if we gave Betty's god-daughter some
supplies
to off-load

ROBYN

Hold up.
Hold up.
You want Betty's twelve-year-old god-daughter
to sell pot brownies for us
to her friends.

SHARON

Or regular pot.

ROBYN

Sharon!

SHARON

To her classmates.

ROBYN

Her classmates?

SHARON
(Helpfully.)
She might not have many actual *friends*
she's a little strange-looking
(Her teeth, and...)
but uh, classmates and
you know, kids she knows from places.

ROBYN

Okay
Sharon?
Okay
listen

SHARON

And I *know* you might have concerns

ROBYN

'concerns'
yes, yes I do
concerns

SHARON

But I just think,
let's think about this.
Expansion is progress.
So. Let's consider.

    A beat.

ROBYN

'Expansion is progress'
Where did you even…?

SHARON

I read that.

ROBYN

You read it.

SHARON

I was reading this article in *Harvard Business Review*
yesterday
about women entrepreneurs
and they all said *Expansion is progress.*
Because women settle for things,
we nurture, nurturing requires settlement
to some degree
but
we deserve progress too.
Don't you think?

> *A beat.*

ROBYN

Since when do you read *Harvard Business Review*?

SHARON

I want to know what's going on.

ROBYN

…by reading *Harvard Business Review*?

SHARON

What!

> *Pause—refocusing:*

ROBYN

Sharon… I don't think off-loading pot brownies to Betty's
adolescent buck-toothed god-daughter is going to provide
progress, entrepreneurial or otherwise. And you know, *low
profile*, Sharon

we are keeping a *low profile*
we are not *expanding* a *business*.
Sustaining and expanding are two different activities
and it's great that now you read *Harvard Business Review*
but expanding is no longer an interest of mine.

    Beat.

SHARON

And then there's this other thing.

ROBYN

What other thing…

SHARON

Well.
I got us something.

ROBYN

What?

SHARON

And it's sort of just in case.
We don't need it *now*
so I don't think we should think that we need it *now*
but I just thought, it's good to be prepared.

ROBYN

What did you buy.

    SHARON goes to a large shopping bag.
    She takes out a large gun.

ROBYN

SHARON.

SHARON

I went to the Walmart in Cedar Rapids

ROBYN

WHAT THE FUCK!

SHARON

and there was a nice young man who [sold me this]

ROBYN

Do you even know how to use a gun??

SHARON

I've been watching videos on YouTube
it doesn't look hard.

ROBYN

Sharon!
We cannot own a gun.

SHARON

This is Iowa, *everybody* owns a gun.

ROBYN

Okay
a hunting rifle
if you hunted
okay
but *this*
sort of phallic
semi-automatic...
what *is* this?

SHARON

Do you wanna hold it?
It's got a weight to it
it feels warm
like you're holding a sort of pet or
somebody's limb
or your own extra limb

ROBYN

Sharon!

SHARON

What?

ROBYN

Take it back.

SHARON

What??

ROBYN

Do you have the receipt?
Take it back.

SHARON
(Canny.)
Hold it and I'll look for the receipt.

A beat.

ROBYN holds the gun.
SHARON knows exactly where her receipt is, and takes her sweet time 'looking' for it.
She watches ROBYN hold the gun.

What's it feel like?

ROBYN

Heavy.

SHARON

Powerful?

ROBYN

Dangerous.

SHARON

But doesn't it feel good?
(Pause.)
I walked out of that Walmart
and I knew that everybody who looked at me
was looking through me
but I knew what they weren't seeing.
I knew what I had.

Beat.

ROBYN

Find your receipt?

SHARON
(Not really looking.)
Still looking.

ROBYN

We're not gonna shoot anybody.
Who did you wanna shoot?

SHARON

I don't want to shoot anybody
I just want to be prepared.

ROBYN

Prepared to shoot?

SHARON

Just prepared.

ROBYN

Take it back. Okay? Sharon?

SHARON

Okay.

ROBYN

Promise?

SHARON

I said okay.
I will.
Robyn, I will.

ROBYN

OK and just
in general, Sharon,
this is not...
expansion...is not...
OK?

SHARON

Okay.

ROBYN

This is just
as this is.
No bigger.

SHARON

No smaller?

ROBYN

Just as we are.

SHARON

I like how we are.

Beat.

Oh! Found it.

ROBYN

Yeah?

SHARON

Right here.

ROBYN

Okay.

SHARON

Are we good?

ROBYN

We're good.

9.

Evening, one week later.
The kitchen.
Music on the record player.

ROBYN stands, with the box of dolls. She has a large garbage bag.
She seems to be about to throw them out, and then...
The sound of SHARON, approaching.
ROBYN hides the box quickly.

SHARON comes into the kitchen from the outside.
She is Dressed. Up.
And a teeny little bit drunk.
And it's pretty hot.

ROBYN

Oh hey look who's home!

SHARON

There you are!

ROBYN
(Taking in the outfit.)
Whoa. Whoa mama.
Look at you.

SHARON

Right? Whaddayou think?

ROBYN

Bold. Bold choice.

SHARON

Right?!

Beat.

Bold good or bold bad?

She grabs a joint off the table, lights it.

ROBYN
Bold is...bold. It exists above the dictates of good and evil.

Beat.

That's for your book club, you *know* we don't smoke that.

SHARON

It's just a little bit.
Do you want me to put this out?

ROBYN

No, just—next time—

    Beat.

SO.

SHARON
(Can't wait to be asked.)

Yeeeees?

ROBYN

How was your date?

SHARON

WELL.

    This is a good thing!

He's an ophthalmologist!

ROBYN

Okay...

SHARON

Eyes, that's eyes.
He knows about eyes.

ROBYN

Yeah okay, eyes.

SHARON
(This is not a good thing...)

He's going bald...

ROBYN

Bald, okay.

SHARON
(Not sure how she feels about this.)
He was a child star?

ROBYN
What kind?

SHARON
Gerber food commercial.

ROBYN
Hmm.

SHARON
His experiences with fame haunted him. To this day.

ROBYN
Fame! Okay!
Overall verdict?

> *Beat.*

SHARON
And he kissed me.

ROBYN
You mean like an end-of-night kiss
or like a Kiss?

SHARON
Well we kissed on the cheek when I first arrived at the
restaurant
but those don't count
(I mean in Paris everybody kisses each other on the cheek *all
the time*)
but *after* dinner
we made out.
In the car.
And he was very passionate
he kept bumping me into things
like the gear shift because he drives stick.

ROBYN

Well done!

SHARON

I don't think I ever really did that as a teenager.
Like, forty years late, I made out in a car.

Beat.

And he put his
hand
on my

Breasts.

you know

ROBYN

Oh-kay, I don't think we need to

SHARON

And he squeezed

ROBYN

Oh-kay

SHARON

And I just thought
is *this* what all the fuss is about?

ROBYN

… What?

SHARON

I just. I don't know. I was bored.

ROBYN

You were making out in a car!
You were banging into the gear shift!
He was squeezing various parts of you!
How were you bored?

SHARON

It just felt like
I don't know
he was so...normal.
He told me I was pretty.
It was very unambiguous.
He had kids, he showed me pictures of them.
They looked like kids.

ROBYN

Sharon! You went on a nice date
with a man who was NOT a serial killer—

SHARON

I sort of just started entertaining myself
after a time.

ROBYN

What does that mean?

> *SHARON takes a series of objects out of her pocket: cigarettes,
> a fancy lighter.*

SHARON

I took these out of his pocket while we were kissing.

ROBYN

You—!

SHARON
(With pride.)

He didn't even notice.

ROBYN

You *robbed* him
while he was *kissing* you.

SHARON

He won't miss them
It's just cigarettes

ROBYN

And a nice lighter!

SHARON

A lighter is a lighter.

ROBYN

That's not the point and you know it.

SHARON

When I was a girl I stole a penny candy from the store
and my mother slapped me across the face.
She said, 'Little girls don't take what isn't theirs.'
And you know what?
She was right.
It takes a grown lady to do that.

Despite herself, ROBYN is laughing.

ROBYN

Sharon!!

SHARON
(Takes out a watch, sets it on the table.)
Right off his wrist, and he didn't notice.
Turns out, I'm good. Who knew!

ROBYN

Sharon!

SHARON

What!

ROBYN

Sharon you *cannot* just
go on dates with people and
mug them

SHARON

He wasn't complaining.

ROBYN

I am complaining! (I think I'm complaining.)
The point is—

SHARON

The point *is*, if you'd been on a date with me
I wouldn't have mugged you.

Beat. The air changes just a little.

ROBYN

What does *that* mean.

SHARON

I just mean
you're more exciting
than the rest of them.
I wouldn't have had to.

Beat.

Are you *mad* at me?

Beat.

He's just a guy
you don't even know him.

Beat. ROBYN is sober now.

ROBYN

Careful. With that.

SHARON

What!

ROBYN

'Just a guy'

SHARON

I mean I didn't *kill* him.
I didn't like, *poison* him.
You know?
Everything's fine.

ROBYN

And the next time you go on a date?
And you get bored?
And it's just a guy?

SHARON

Don't you think you're overreacting?

Beat.

ROBYN

I meant to give this up.
I really did.
Until you, I did.

SHARON

Oh…

ROBYN

Until you
and how it was so
fun
and how you
surprised me
(*You always surprise me*)
until *that*
I really
really
did.

SHARON

… Thank you.

ROBYN

It's hard to go back to the normal world.
To getting what you want so slowly, over so much time,
or sometimes to never getting it at all.
You start to need this.

SHARON

I'm doing this for fun.

ROBYN

Or you want it so bad it feels like you need it.

SHARON

I don't *need* it, Robyn.

ROBYN

Are you sure?

Beat. SHARON is NOT sure.

SHARON
(Quiet.)

I'm not a kid who doesn't know right from wrong.
You aren't raising me. Somebody already raised me, and they
did a shitty job
and then I raised somebody and I did a shitty job
and you, generally, all you've done is be a really
really
great
roommate.

Beat.

*ROBYN almost laughs, but also she's too sad to laugh. SHARON
tries to make out her expression.*

Robyn.

ROBYN

What.

SHARON

Don't be sad.
Are you sad?
Don't be sad.

ROBYN
(Means it.)

I'm glad you had a good date.

SHARON

Fuck that.
I don't care about that.

ROBYN

Sharon...

SHARON

I've had a good month. With you.
I've had good coffee
good conversations
and now we're making good money and that's good
but actually, it's not the money, it's the *making*.
Making something with you.

ROBYN

Sharon...

SHARON

I look forward to waking up in the morning.
Everything is a Yes.
I'm smarter and faster and
younger
than I knew I could be.
Don't be sad. I can't remember ever having been this happy.

A beat and then SHARON gets up decisively.

We are gonna dance.

ROBYN

Oh come on.

SHARON

No
No
We are gonna dance.
You can't go to bed sad.

She puts on a record. It might be Sydney Bechet's 'Si Tu Vois Ma Mere'.

ROBYN

What *is* that.

SHARON

It's World War Two London.
The whole world has been bombed.

ROBYN

London?

SHARON

We're the only two people left, in the ruins of a building
that has *also* been bombed but still, oddly, is standing.
You're a pickpocket. And I'm a soldier.
Or maybe I'm a pickpocket and you're a sailor.
I don't know.

ROBYN
(But laughing.)

You're crazy.

SHARON

We're sheltering. From the cold cold English wind.
And then suddenly
from somewhere far away
a lone apartment somewhere high off the street
we hear music.
It drifts.
It comes to us.
It catches us.

ROBYN

And then what?

*SHARON takes ROBYN's hand. They dance. Old school WW2
bombed-out London dance. It's playful and funny at first, and
then it's quieter, and then it's tender and sweet and kind of
shy, and then it heats up. And then SHARON kisses ROBYN.*

A beat. ROBYN pulls away. Wide-eyed.

A moment between them.

SHARON

I'm sorry.

Silence.

I'm so sorry.

Silence.

Should I be sorry?

ROBYN

I have to go to bed.

SHARON

Are you mad at me?

ROBYN

I have to go to bed.

Beat.

I'm not mad at you.

SHARON

Robyn...

ROBYN

Good night.

10.

Late morning. Sunlight slants in.
The kitchen, as they left it: a mess.

SHARON comes downstairs in her bathrobe, groggy, a little hung-over.

She puts the coffee on.
Starts to clean up a little.
She's waiting for ROBYN.
She goes to the stairs, listens to see if ROBYN is awake yet.
She starts making a little extra noise to see if Robyn will wake up.
Dropping things, 'accidentally'.

Still nothing.

And then she sees a note.
She picks it up.
Reads it.
Can't quite wrap her mind around it.

She opens the cabinets. ROBYN's things are gone. Out to the porch - ROBYN's boxes are gone. She rushes to look out onto the driveway. ROBYN's car is gone. She comes back inside.

A beat.

She sits down heavily at the kitchen table.

A beat.

She picks the note back up.
Reads it.
Crumples it.
She makes a phone call. It goes to voicemail.

SHARON

Robyn, hi.
This is Sharon.
Obviously.
I just woke up and I saw your things are all gone and
did we get robbed in the night? I just got worried
so
call me.

JEN SILVERMAN

Beat.

Actually I got your note, so

Beat.

call me anyway.

Beat.

You didn't have to…[leave]

Beat.

I mean if it was—you know—
I was drunk and I *barely* remember what I was even [doing]
and it's not like I'm *even* [gay]
but even if I *was* [gay]
it's not like I want to date you
so
you don't have to worry about that!
There's lots of other women I'd date
if I was going to date a woman
so…

Beat, disentangling herself.

Call me.
OK?

She hangs up.

Beat.

She calls ROBYN again. Voicemail.

Hi Robyn it's me again
clearly
you probably aren't checking your phone
and you're probably going to check it sometime soon
sometime later
but soon
and then you'll see I've been trying to reach you
and I'm sorry if I'm being alarmist

but
it's pretty
empty.
The house.
Is empty.
And I just.
I think you should call me?
So.

 This is raw.

I miss you.

 Attempting to recover.

OK.
Bye.

 She hangs up.

 Beat.

 She calls ROBYN again. Voicemail.

If you're going to leave because I kissed you?
That's bullshit.
And if you're leaving for some other reason?
That's also bullshit.
I am a grown-ass adult.
Okay.
If you just don't want to be *responsible* for me,
then don't worry!
You're not responsible!
I absolve you!
And if you don't want to do the things we were doing
the phone calls and the book club weed-ring and whatever
that's fine!
Don't do it!
I won't do it!
I don't care, I'm done anyway.
Or if I did it, I'd do it without you!
And where are you going to go, anyway?

Nobody wants you.
Amanda doesn't want you!
So come back!

    She hangs up.
    She finds a small box under things.
    ROBYN's ceramic dolls.
    She takes one out.
    Emotion surges in her.
    She smashes the doll.
    That felt good. Another one. Another one.
    Then freezes.
    Inside the third doll is a small plastic bag.
    The ceramic doll was stuffed with coke.
    Another one of ROBYN's businesses.
    She smashes more dolls. More bags of coke.
    Coke and doll-shards everywhere,
    SHARON is frozen in this moment of discovery.

11.

The kitchen.
Morning. A week later.

SHARON sleeps in her kitchen.
Filth has accumulated. Dishes are unwashed, maybe take-out cartons litter the floor, clothes strewn. The WW2 London record has been playing on loop but now the record spins and the needle scratches.

The phone rings. SHARON jolts awake. She looks terrible. Not entirely sober. It goes to the answering machine. SHARON's recorded voice on the machine is perky and bright.

ANSWERING MACHINE

Hiii, you've reached Sharon, I'm so sorry I can't come to the phone right now but leave me a message at the beep! Have a great day!

SHARON'S SON

Mom. Hey. It's me.
You home?

> *SHARON makes no move to answer it.*

Haven't heard from you in a while.
I mean that's cool, you must be
Doing Things so
that's awesome!
But
Your roommate called me.

> *Will she pick up? But...no.*
> *He can't help her right now.*

She said she had to leave for business
and she wanted me to check in on you
and I realised, we hadn't talked in a bit
like a little bit
and uh
you left me some messages?
That, frankly, were kind of

crazy messages?
so I thought…
I'd call you
but
I guess I'll try you later.
Bye mom.

He hangs up.

A beat.

And then, the phone rings again.
This time, she answers it.

SHARON

… Hello…?

And we see ROBYN. Perhaps by the side of a highway. Perhaps somewhere shadowy and too far to reach. Either way, her voice fills the entire space, soft and close.

ROBYN

Hello. This is Victoria Jones from the Franco-Global Society of International Orphans. Is this Sharon?

A beat.

SHARON

This is Sharon.

ROBYN

Hi Sharon.
I'm calling you because we want to thank you.
For your hard work.
Your…donations. Your…support.

SHARON

My…?

ROBYN

We recognise that it is hard to…care for strangers.
People who maybe
their lives have taken place on the other side of the world from you

and their lives will continue to take place on the other side of
the world
and someone with a less...developed...heart
might think: *what does that have to do with me.*
But you cared. You are a caring person.
And the Franco-Global Society of International Orphans just
wants to thank you for that.

    A beat.

SHARON

Are you coming back?

ROBYN

Orphans, once they have left their homes for new placements
rarely return.

SHARON

Victoria Jones.

ROBYN

Yes?

SHARON

Why is that.

ROBYN

Because sometimes their pasts are
contentious
and they recognise that they could cause great harm
to those they have come to care for
by returning.

SHARON

Or maybe sometimes they forget and move on and don't care
anymore.

ROBYN

No. That's not it.
I've done this job for a hundred years.
And that's not it.

SHARON

Are you with Amanda?

A beat.

ROBYN

I have to go now, Sharon, but
on behalf of all of us here at FGSIO
please take care of yourself.

SHARON

Wait!

ROBYN

What is it?

SHARON

Will I ever hear from you again?

A beat.

ROBYN

We might occasionally make a courtesy call,
to check in on some of our most helpful donors.

A beat.

SHARON

Bye Victoria Jones.

ROBYN

Goodbye.

She hangs up. A beat.

SHARON looks around her kitchen.
She starts to wake up in a way.
This is a prayer. Or a poem.
It is raw and fragile and new.

SHARON

I'm standing in my kitchen.

I am standing in my kitchen and

my roommate told me that
people find words for themselves but
those words are not always right and

I think I don't have the right words, anymore.

Sharon doesn't feel   [right]
Wife is no longer   [right]
and for some time now, Mother has not been
right.

    Pause.

'Roommate' was good.
That was a good word.
But now it's no longer
right.

    Beat—a burst of anger.

I just think
that there is a better way to do things
than the one where we live a certain life
and then we lose it completely!

    Pause.

I slept in the kitchen for a week.
And now I'm awake.
And this house is very empty.
And I don't know where to start.
Except over. Again.

    She gathers up the doll-shards and coke baggies. We might
    think she's going to throw them out.
    And then...
    She sets the bags of coke all on the table in a long row.

           JEN SILVERMAN

All first poems are bad poems…
but there's a great liberty in being bad.

As she considers her loot, and a glorious future of illegal activity…

Blackout.

End of play.

COLLECTIVE RAGE: A PLAY IN 5 BETTIES

IN ESSENCE, A QUEER AND OCCASIONALLY
HAZARDOUS EXPLORATION; DO YOU REMEMBER
WHEN YOU WERE IN MIDDLE SCHOOL AND YOU
READ ABOUT SHACKLETON AND HOW HE EXPLORED
THE ANTARCTIC?; IMAGINE THE ANTARCTIC AS A
PUSSY AND IT'S SORT OF LIKE THAT

Special thanks to Dane Laffrey, who essentially commissioned a treatise on queer love and queer rage, and got this fantasia instead, and to Basil Kreimendahl, who is always workin' on that truck.

COLLECTIVE RAGE: A PLAY IN 5 BETTIES premiered at Woolly Mammoth Theatre Company in September 2016. It was directed by Mike Donahue, set design by Dane Laffrey, costumes by Kelsey Hunt, lighting by Colin K. Bills, sound by Thomas Sowers, song composition by Daniel Kluger, and dramaturgy by Kirsten Bowen. The cast was as follows:

BETTY 1	Beth Hylton
BETTY 2	Dorea Schmidt
BETTY 3	Natascia Diaz
BETTY 4	Kate Rigg
BETTY 5	Felicia Curry

COLLECTIVE RAGE: A PLAY IN 5 BETTIES had its UK premiere at Southwark Playhouse, produced by Antic Face and Nik Holttum Productions in January 2018. It was directed by Charlie Parham, design by Anna Reid, lighting by Zoe Spurr, sound by Hollie Buhagiar, and movement by Nichola Treherne. The cast was as follows:

BETTY 1	Sara Stewart
BETTY 2	Lucy McCormick
BETTY 3	Beatriz Romilly
BETTY 4	Johnnie Fiori
BETTY 5	Genesis Lynea

CAST: THE BETTIES

BETTY 1 — Femme, white, rich, uptight,
fueled by secret rage

BETTY 2 — Femme, white or Asian, rich,
uptight but coming undone

BETTY 3 — Femme, Latina, charismatic
and pretty, kind of a know-it-all

BETTY 4 — Butch lesbian, any ethnicity
great tattoos, gently melancholic,
is too often ignored

BETTY 5 — Genderqueer (masculine-of-center),
any ethnicity, great tattoos, owns a
hole-in-the-wall boxing gym

TIME

Now.

PLACE

New York?

NOTES ON THE TEXT

Scene titles: The scene titles are probably best projected but they might be announced before each scene by somebody with a God mic. (If so, it's best to have a female voice announcing them).

On casting: Casting is best when racially diverse. Whenever possible, Betties 3, 4 and 5 should be different ethnicities from each other. Betties 1 and 5 must not be the same ethnicity.

On design: The space is very fluid. The pace is fast and sometimes breakneck. Scene changes should be immediate and uncluttered by props, until the second-to-last party scene, which can take more time.

[ ] is unspoken, although the character is thinking it.

( ) is spoken out loud but is a side thought.

MOST IMPORTANTLY

Despite the comedy, the Betties are in desperate pursuit of happiness, in the face of an almost unbearable loneliness. Do not eschew the human, raw, and sad in favour of the funny—even if you think the text is giving permission. (It isn't.) The humor works best when we genuinely care about all five women—and when they learn to genuinely care about each other.

1. BETTY 1 IS IN A RAGE

BETTY 1 walks out on stage.
The space is very empty and very spare.
She looks very proper. But she's pissed off.

BETTY 1

I was watching the news the other day and
there was this segment on mutilated children?
And then I was watching the news, and
there was this special insider report on amputees.
And then I was watching the news and
it told me that I was going to die of diabetes and high blood
pressure and lyme disease and ovarian cancer and
violent-thug-attack by a person, I think a Man? A Foreign Man?
—oh maybe that's racist.
Well that's just the news, I am not responsible for the news.

This world is terrible. This world is awful.
I am Very Very Concerned about the State of Things.
My husband Richard came home and I said to him RICHARD
I said RICHARD
I am Very Very Concerned About The State of Things.
My husband Richard is a calm person.
He is a logical and a rational person and He Wears A Suit.
And Richard said to me: BETTY
Richard said: BETTY
Richard said: Betty, Don't Worry.

Pause—with sudden fury.

AND THAT DIDN'T MAKE ME FEEL BETTER.

Beat—breath—with great dignity.

There is currently nothing in the whole world
that makes me feel better.
So I decided to throw a Dinner Party.

2. BETTIES 1 AND 2 AT A DINNER PARTY

BETTY 2 walks out onstage.
She's younger and a little more fragile. Possibly coming unraveled.

Now all of a sudden the two BETTIES are having a dinner party.
A really uptight dinner party, where they pretend to be much
better friends than they actually are.

BETTY 1

Betty.

BETTY 2

Yes Betty?

BETTY 1

Lady, I love your nails.

BETTY 2

Thanks lady, I love your nails too.

BETTY 1

I think that colour is just darling on you. Where'd you get it?

BETTY 2

Well I went to this little salon on the Upper East.
Charles said, *You treat yourself, you just treat yourself.*
So I just treated myself.

BETTY 1

That Charles. He's so thoughtful.

BETTY 2

I *know*!

BETTY 1

Richard gave me the nicest present the other day.

BETTY 2

What was that?

BETTY 1

Well I'd been so Stressed out, I've just been feeling a lot of Stress
and I came home and Richard's assistant had gotten me a gift
card for a massage

Richard told his assistant to get me a gift card for a massage
isn't that thoughtful?

BETTY 2

That's so thoughtful.

An awkward beat. They sip their white wine.

BETTY 1

How are the kids?

BETTY 2

I don't have kids.

BETTY 1

Oh!
I thought...?

BETTY 2

No...

BETTY 1

Oh.

They sip.

BETTY 2

This neighbourhood is so lovely.

BETTY 1

That's so true.
Other neighbourhoods are so much less lovely these days.

BETTY 2

Oh, I know...

BETTY 1

They say there's an Influx
if you know what I mean
yes, that's certainly happening.

Beat.

I didn't mean to be...   [racist]
I hope that wasn't...?   [racist]

BETTY 2

… No?

BETTY 1

Because that has nothing to do with it.
In fact, some of our Best Friends are People of Colour.

BETTY 2

… They are?

BETTY 1

For example, Betty, whom I have also invited to dinner tonight.

BETTY 2

Which Betty?

BETTY 1

She had a hard childhood but she has risen above it with resilience
and courage.
She's sassy and no-nonsense.
She's a nurse or a healthcare worker.
Or somebody's nanny? Maybe she's *my* nanny?

BETTY 2

You don't have a nanny because you don't have kids either.

BETTY 1

Oh. That's right, I met her at Sephora!
Here she is!

> *BETTY 3 walks out onstage.*
> *She's Latina, high-femme, super queer.*
> *She sits down with them. The dinner party is now in full swing.*

BETTY 3

The first time I fucked a girl I was like
BINGO! I WON! I WON THE FUCKING LOTTERY!
I was all up in that shit!
I was like, girl, you come here
you put your mouth here
to the left! to the right!
It was the wild west up in there!

I was like a pro-wrestler and a cowboy
and also like an astronaut
like the Neil fuckin' Armstrong of the bedroom.

   Beat.

BETTY 1

That's not good conversation for a dinner party.

BETTY 3

No?

BETTY 1 and 2

No.

BETTY 3

How come?

BETTY 1

We don't talk about sex at dinner parties.

BETTY 3

What else you talk about?

BETTY 2

We aren't having sex, so we can't talk about it.

BETTY 3

Maybe you should start having it.

BETTY 1
(This should be obvious.)

We're married.

   Reclaiming the dinner party convo.

How's Charles' job?

BETTY 2

I think he's going to get a promotion.

BETTY 1

That's so exciting. So well deserved.

                    BETTY 2
He works so hard all the time.

                    BETTY 1
I know!

                    BETTY 2
And Richard?

                    BETTY 1
He's managing a brand new account.

                    BETTY 2
That's wonderful.

                    BETTY 1
It's a big one. Lots of room for upward mobility.

                    BETTY 2
Richard is such an achiever.

                    BETTY 1
So is Charles.

   They beam at each other uncomfortably.

                    BETTY 3
Can I talk about pussy?

                    BETTY 1
              (Through her beaming smile.)
We said No.

                    BETTY 3
Not like *using* the pussy, not *activating* the pussy
just pussy itself.

                    BETTY 1
No and we don't like that word, pussy. It's indecent.

                    BETTY 3
What about pussy lips?
Just the lips around the pussy?

BETTY 1

Absolutely not.

BETTY 3

This is a boring-ass dinner party.

BETTY 1

That. Is the *point*. Of a *dinner party*.

BETTY 3

Oh.
Okay.
Well.
In that case,
I'm gonna throw my own dinner party.

BETTY 1

You do that.

BETTY 2

(Whispering to her.)

What time is it and where?

3. BETTY 3 HAS HER OWN DINNER PARTY,
IN WHICH ALL OF US TALK ABOUT PUSSY

BETTIES 3 and 2.

Also a new BETTY: BETTY 4, who has awesome tattoos and is as butch as you can get. She is in love with BETTY 3, despite being friend-zoned. BETTY 3 tells us the story of her day.

BETTY 3

—And then the bitch was all, 'I don't know, lemme try the Givenchy tester.' And I was like, 'You been trying testers for ninety minutes, now it's time to buy.' And the bitch was all, 'This is a free country' and I was all, 'NOT IF YOU GOT MY FUCKIN' JOB.'

Beat.

Sephora gets cray.

BETTY 2

Oh wow.

BETTY 4

You handle things really well.

BETTY 3

That fuckin' place gives me hives.

BETTY 4

I go visit her at work and she handles stress really well.

BETTY 3

I need to quit.

BETTY 4
(A little alarmed.)

Quit?

BETTY 3
(Already moving on.)

… Anyway, then I went to Party City and I got banners for the dinner party but then on the way home I got into a fight on the subway and I forgot them under my seat.

BETTY 2

You got in a fight??

BETTY 3

Bitch pushed me.

BETTY 2

The same bitch?

BETTY 3

No! A different bitch!

BETTY 4
(In solidarity.)

Bitches are bitches.

BETTY 2

Wow. I don't think I've ever been in a fight.

BETTY 3 and 4

Never?

BETTY 2

If somebody pushes me I say, 'Sorry', even though I was the
one who got pushed?
And whenever I ask anybody to do anything for me, even if
they're a waiter, I say, 'Sorry,' even if it's their job? And then
after they've done it, or even before they've done it, or actually
even if they never do it at all, I say, 'Thank you'?

   Beat.

BETTY 3

And she's not having sex.

BETTY 4

Damn.

BETTY 2
(Horrified and embarrassed.)

Betty!!

BETTY 4

That sucks.

BETTY 3

I KNOW!

BETTY 4

How long's it been?

BETTY 2

Betty!!

BETTY 3

I feel like the longest I've ever gone is…

She thinks.

Three days!

Pause.

I guess it was two.

Pause.

But actually I cheated so I guess it was one.

BETTY 4
(To BETTY 2.)
Her girlfriend was out of town but she met a sailor.

BETTY 3

If you put it in a uniform, I'm gonna tap that shit.

BETTY 2

Wow. I feel like
it's so strange to even talk about this.

BETTY 3
(A realisation, to BETTY 4.)
How'd you know about the sailor?

BETTY 4

You got wasted and told me about him.

BETTY 3

Oh yeahhh.

To BETTY 2.

So what about you?

BETTY 2

Wow.
This is so…!
I've never had any friends before.

BETTY 4 and 3

Whoa. / Ayy…

BETTY 2

This is so exciting!
Well I guess
it's been like five years? Maybe six?
And
Charles is very nice.
He's very considerate?
We read in bed together?
Like, he's on his side of the bed? And he reads *Hunting & Fishing*.
And I'm on my side of the bed? And I read *Ladies Home Journal*.

BETTY 4

What's that?

BETTY 3

Porn?

BETTY 2

No, it's a *journal* about *ladies* who want to make a *home*.
It's just…suggestions.
For how to do things better than how you're doing them.

BETTY 4

That sounds depressing.

BETTY 3

She needs to get laid. We gotta help her with that.

BETTY 2

Oh no, you don't have to…

BETTY 4

Shut up, we're helping you with that.

BETTY 3 passes out hand-mirrors.

BETTY 2

Uh…what's that for?

BETTY 3

We're gonna look at pussy
so you know what you got to work with.

BETTY 2

I don't think I'm gay?

BETTY 3

I'm bi.

BETTY 4

I'm queer.

BETTY 2

I don't think I'm either?

BETTY 3

Are you currently right now having sex at this juncture?

BETTY 2

Uh…no?

BETTY 3

Then you don't got enough data…and the window of potential
is open.

BETTY 4

Wide open.

BETTY 3

(Leering a little.)

Wide.

BETTY 2

Oh. Oh wow.

BETTY 3
(Officiating.)

Place the hand-mirror below your vaginal situation.
In a pussy-specific area.
Two inches from your cooch-ular region.
Then look.

BETTY 4
(Looking.)

Okay.

BETTY 3
(Looking.)

Mmmm!

BETTY 4
(Trying to glimpse BETTY 3's mirror.)

Hmm…

BETTY 3
(Unaware, and enjoying herself.)

Mmmm-hmmm!!

To BETTY 2.

You're not looking.

BETTY 2

I'm scared.

BETTY 4

What are you scared of?

BETTY 2

Something terrible might be there.

BETTY 3

It's just your cho-cha.

BETTY 2

What if it's ugly? What if there's teeth? What if it's lopsided?
What if it's lumpy? Or flat? Or geometrically displeasing?
Or what if I don't have one at all and there's just a small animal

who lives there, like a lizard or a dwarf hamster, and all I see are the gleam of its little eyes as it stares back up at me?

A beat. They consider this.

BETTY 4

Everybody has a pussy.

BETTY 3

Nobody has a hamster.

BETTY 4

But if you did, it might be nice.

BETTY 3

Nothing is going to get better for you if you can't open your eyes.

BETTY 2

Maybe everything is fine for me right now.

BETTY 3

Look at her.

They both look at her. A judgemental gaze.

BETTY 2

What!!

BETTY 4

Yeah.

BETTY 3

Oh yeah.

BETTY 4

Bleak.

BETTY 3

Pretty bleak.

BETTY 4

Depressing.

BETTY 2

You guys!!

BETTY 3

Look at your pussy, Betty.

BETTY 4

Both eyes.

BETTY 2 looks at her pussy in the hand-mirror. A long beat.

BETTY 3

Well??

BETTY 4

What do you think?

BETTY 3

What's down there?

BETTY 2

Oh.

BETTY 3 and 4

What??

BETTY 2

Ohhhh…

BETTY 3 and 4

What!

BETTY 2 experiences a moment of extreme self-actualisation and sexual awakening.

BETTY 2

OH…

Pause.

I have to go home now.

Hand-mirror in hand.

Can I keep this? I'm keeping this.

She leaves.

BETTY 3

I always throw the *best* dinner parties!

4. BETTIES 4 AND 5 WORK ON THEIR TRUCKS
AND DISCUSS LOVE

BETTY 4 with a new BETTY, BETTY 5. BETTY 5 is equally butch and has EVEN MORE awesome tattoos. BETTY 5 is wildly charismatic and if you were a lady, even a straight lady, you'd get fluttery.

They work on their trucks side by side.

BETTY 4

Been fixing my truck.

BETTY 5

I can see.

BETTY 4

Gettin' all up in there. Engine was busted. Been fixin' it up.

BETTY 5

Looks good.

BETTY 4

I see you gotta new truck.

BETTY 5

Yeah.

BETTY 4

Didn't wanna fix your old one?

BETTY 5

Figured it was time for a new one.

BETTY 4

Wow, okay.
I see that.

    Beat, they work.

Looks like you got some new ink.

BETTY 5

Yeah.

BETTY 4

Cool, yeah. It looks great.

BETTY 5

Thanks man.

BETTY 4
(Has to ask.)

You didn't wanna just keep your old ink?

BETTY 5

Felt like it was time for some new ink.

BETTY 4

No, yeah, sure.
Where'd you get it?

BETTY 5

Prison.

BETTY 4

Oh!
Cool.

BETTY 5

You should go to prison sometime. It's great.

BETTY 4

Oh yeah?

BETTY 5

Yeah!
There were a lot of activities. And I was the best at the activities.
And there were a lot of straight girls. And they all had crushes
on me.
Oh yeah, and then I got to work in the machine shop.

BETTY 4
(Increasingly sad.)

Oh wow that sounds fun.
That sounds like you had a really good time

BETTY 5

Yeah the machine shop was rad
and then I met these hot chicks who did meth
and they had a smuggling ring?
and I was really good at smuggling.

This bit really matters to her.

And my best friend in prison was this chick
who had serious gambling problems
and we played a lot of cards.

BETTY 4

Oh wow.

BETTY 5

And she told me I was a natural.
She was like, 'You're a natural.'
And I was like, 'Thanks.'

BETTY 4
(Sad.)
That's really great that you made so many new friends
that's awesome and I'm really happy for you.

BETTY 5
(Also suddenly sad.)
Yeah...

*A moment. BETTIES 4 and 5 clock that the other one is sad,
but neither knows why or what to do about it.*

BETTY 4

I've called you.

BETTY 5

Yeah?

BETTY 4

Since you got out. Yeah. I've been calling.

BETTY 5

Yeah I haven't really been answering the phone.

BETTY 4

Yeah I noticed.

BETTY 5

Ever since I got out, all I want to do is work on my truck.
And eat pussy.
And run my boxing gym. And eat pussy.

BETTY 4

Yeah no it's cool. I barely even noticed.

BETTY 5

You eating any new pussy?

BETTY 4

Me? Yeah totally.

BETTY 5

Who is it?

BETTY 4

Just somebody you don't know.

BETTY 5

… Or are you still hung up on Betty?

BETTY 4

I don't know what you mean.

BETTY 5

Sephora Betty with the tits Betty, who we grew up with Betty.

BETTY 4

We're just very very close friends.

BETTY 5

Yeah okay.

BETTY 4

I don't feel like that about her at all.

BETTY 5

Yeah okay.

BETTY 4

Anyway, what about you? Who are you...with?

BETTY 5

Pussy is pussy. You don't gotta name it.

They work.

BETTY 4

She says she wants to quit Sephora.

BETTY 5

Good.

BETTY 4

I don't know.

BETTY 5

She should try something new. She should go to prison!

A beat. They work.

BETTY 4

Betty?

BETTY 5

Ssup, Betty.

BETTY 4

I feel like
things
are changing.

BETTY 5

I hope so.

BETTY 4

But everything was good the way it was.
Wasn't it?

BETTY 5

Change is exciting.

BETTY 4

Change is sad.
Change is things getting forgotten.
Change is people getting left behind.

BETTY 5 looks at BETTY 4 closely.
A long level glance.

BETTY 5

You good, right?

BETTY 4
(Lying.)

Me? Yeah. I'm great.
You?

BETTY 5
(Lying.)

Great.

5. BETTY 1 HAS MORE RAGE,
AND DOES SOMETHING ABOUT IT

BETTY 1

I was watching the News again this morning and
there was this Special on placental abruptions
and then I was watching the News and there was an interview
with a woman who was buried underground for twelve years
and she's alive!! But her stomach shriveled up so they had to
remove it
and *then* I watched this report on octogenarians who commit
suicide
because life was *just* so disappointing and
then Richard came home and I said to him: Richard, I said,
Something Has To Be Done. This Is A Terrible Place To Live.
And he said, *The Upper East Side isn't so bad.*
And I said, I Mean The World, Richard.
And he said, *The world is the world, whattaya gonna do.*
What Are You Going To Do?
What Are You Going TO DO??
I AM GOING TO FIGHT BACK, RICHARD!!!!!

   A beat. A deep breath.

So I went to a new gym, it's above 72nd Street so nobody
I know would ever go there, I went to a new gym and I found
a trainer and I said: You Teach Me How To Box.

   *BETTY 5 walks on. Boxing gloves. Showing off her amazing
   tattoos.*

BETTY 5

You?

BETTY 1

Is there a problem?

BETTY 5

You...wanna box?

BETTY 1

Do you have a problem with that, if I want to box?

BETTY 5

You don't look like the sort of person who wants to box.

BETTY 1

Where's your manager.

BETTY 5

I'm the manager. This is my gym.

BETTY 1

Oh.

   A beat.

Listen, young man. Young lady? Young man?

   Breath.

Young lady!

BETTY 5

I'm genderqueer, but whatever.

BETTY 1

I want to learn how to box. And I have A LOT of money. And you are going to teach me. Do you understand?

BETTY 5

You look like you'd cry if I hit you.

BETTY 1

I want to rip someone's throat out. I want to tear out someone's heart muscle with my bare hands. I am not interested in crying.

   BETTY 5 sizes her up anew. Interesting.
   A current of electricity builds from here.

BETTY 5

You got my attention.

BETTY 1
         (Surprised and pleased.)

Oh.

BETTY 5

That sounds more like... Muay Thai?

BETTY 1

... I don't know what that is.

BETTY 5

Krav Maga?

BETTY 1

I've never heard of it.

BETTY 5

Or a particularly stealth and vicious form of karate.

BETTY 1

I've heard of karate.

BETTY 5

Or maybe all of those things all rolled together. Like UFC.

BETTY 1

Yes! Teach me all of the things together!

BETTY 5

Who did you say you were again?

BETTY 1

I'm very rich.
And very powerful.
And very impatient.
And very rich.
And very unhappy.
And very frustrated.
And very gluten-free.
And very vegetarian.
And very alcoholic.
And also still very rich.
Are you a boy or a girl?

BETTY 5

I'm a gender-non-conforming masculine-presenting female-bodied individual. But I'm comfortable with female pronouns.

BETTY 1

(A little flustered.)

I...don't know what any of that means.

BETTY 5

I'm the person who's gonna teach you how to fight.

6. BETTIES 3 AND 4 DISCOVER THAT HIGHBROW THINGS ARE JUST THINGS THAT SEEM TO BE ABOUT OTHER THINGS WHEN THEY'RE ACTUALLY ABOUT PUSSY

BETTY 4 works on her truck.
BETTY 3 drinks Fanta and watches her.

BETTY 3

I went to a play the other night. In The Thea-Tah.

BETTY 4

What'd you do that for?

BETTY 3

I went on a date
with this rich white lady, her husband was outta town
and she took me to The Thea-Tah.
You should go sometime. To The Thea-Tah.

BETTY 4

I'm workin' on my truck.

BETTY 3

You can work on your truck whenever you want, you can only
see the play in The Thea-Tah at specific times.

BETTY 4

You've never asked me to go with you. So.

BETTY 3
(Doesn't clock this.)
It was very complicated BUT
it was about these people who fell in love with each other
and they did terrible things to make sure that nobody loved
anybody else
and then other people put on a play
inside of the first play.

BETTY 4

That sounds confusing.

BETTY 3

It was cultural.

BETTY 4

Whatsit called?

BETTY 3

Summer's Midnight Dream.

BETTY 4

Was Summer the main character?

BETTY 3

There wasn't really a main character.

BETTY 4

That sounds confusing. I like stories where there's a main character and you think something is gonna happen and then it happens. Those are the stories I like.

BETTY 3

This was very famous, lots of people think it's good.

BETTY 4

Like there's this one story with a guy with a dog in a truck. And you know he's gonna drive the truck real fast and there'll be like a view, like some kind of a view, and the dog will hang its head out the window, and then the guy will look at the camera and smile. And then those things happen, and I feel good.

BETTY 3

That's not a story. That's a commercial.

BETTY 4

It's a commercial story.

BETTY 3

You should come with me to The Thea-Tah.

BETTY 4

With you?

BETTY 3

Sometime. Unless I'm on a date.

BETTY 4
(Bristling.)

It sounds boring.
I bet you were bored. Don't lie. Were you bored?

BETTY 3

My mind wandered. It may have wandered.
But I was there. I was present.

BETTY 4

Yeah well my mind can wander in front of my TV and at least
I didn't pay fifty bucks for it.

BETTY 3

Eighty-five.

BETTY 4

EIGHTY-FIVE????

BETTY 3
(Now she's a little ashamed.)

It was cultural.

BETTY 4

My asshole is cultural. I'm not payin' eighty-five dollars for
anything that won't go on my truck.

A beat. They both reflect on this.

BETTY 3
(A quiet confession.)

It wasn't really in English.

BETTY 4

Was it Spanish?

BETTY 3

No, it was like, in kind of an English? But not an English
anybody speaks?

BETTY 4

You're gonna pay eighty-five bucks to go someplace where
you don't understand what they're saying? That's stupid. I can
go to Queens for free in my truck.

BETTY 3

Lots of people liked it.

BETTY 4

Lots of people are stupid.

BETTY 3
(Wistful.)
Everybody stood up and clapped though.
All these old white people stood up and clapped.
And the actors came back onstage and they stood there
and they looked so happy.
Everybody just stared at them and loved them and wanted
to be them—but nobody was.

Wistful, vulnerable.

Hey.

BETTY 4

What.

BETTY 3

You think I could be an actor?

BETTY 4

Sure. You're hot. Sure.

BETTY 3
(Suddenly shy.)
But am I talented?

BETTY 4

I've never seen you act.

BETTY 3

You saw me lie to the cop that one time
when he was like, 'Did you run that red light'
and I was like 'No', and then I cried. And he let us go.

BETTY 4

Oh yeah! That's right.

BETTY 3

So you saw me act that time.

BETTY 4

I thought you were just having a nervous breakdown.

BETTY 3

I think that's sort of what acting is? Only you do it at specific times, on a stage?

BETTY 4

Oh!
Well
then
yeah
you'd be a good actor.

BETTY 3

(This means something to her.)
Thank you.

An awkward beat.

BETTY 4

(Regretting this the second she's said it.)
Or you could be a porn star.

BETTY 3

Betty!

BETTY 4

Sorry. I just meant. Uh. I don't know what I meant.

BETTY 3

My PUSSY is not gonna do the acting, *I* am gonna do the acting. In THE THEA-TAH. People are gonna come and stare at my feelings, and those feelings will be Art.

BETTY 4

(With great philosophical conviction.)
I think a lotta things that seem like art are maybe actually just about pussy.

JEN SILVERMAN

And then also, things that are mostly about pussy might actually be about art.

BETTY 3

That might be true.

Beat.

BETTY 4

… You think I could be an actor?

BETTY 3

You??

BETTY 4

Me.

BETTY 3

I don't know, are you a good liar?

BETTY 4

I dunno.

BETTY 3

Like, remember your ex-girlfriend. Did you ever lie to her?

BETTY 4

I guess, sure.

BETTY 3

Then yeah I don't see why not, you could be an actor.

Beat. They both think about this.

BETTY 4

We should do a play. Together.

BETTY 3

Do we know any plays?

BETTY 4

Well. There's the play you just saw.

BETTY 3

(Getting excited.)

And there was a play inside that play! So that's two plays.

BETTY 4

Maybe we could charge people eighty-five bucks. And I could fix up my truck.

BETTY 3

I could get my hair done.

BETTY 4

New ignition. Muffler. Radio. We'd just drive around playin' tunes.

BETTY 3

I could quit my job.

BETTY 4

We could go on vacation!

BETTY 3

I wanna be the director.

BETTY 4

We could see each other every day.

BETTY 3

And also the writer and also the lead.

BETTY 4

We could have brainstorming sessions late at night.

BETTY 3

And also I'ma do hair and make-up.

BETTY 4

We could really do something. You and me.

BETTY 3

I'm gonna quit Sephora and dedicate my life to The Thea-Tah.

7. BETTY 2 ACTS OUT HER FEELINGS WITH A PUPPET BECAUSE SHE HAS NO REAL FRIENDS

BETTY 2 is alone. She uses her pointer and thumb to make a mouth. Now she has a friend! Her puppet's voice is high-pitched and relentlessly cheerful, no matter what it's saying.

BETTY 2
I went to a dinner party and there were lesbians there.

BETTY 2
They're everywhere these days.

I guess so.

BETTY 2
You better be careful.

BETTY 2
I guess so.

BETTY 2
What did they make you do?

BETTY 2
They made me look at my...you know.

BETTY 2
No, I don't know.

BETTY 2
My...*you* know!

BETTY 2
No, I'm not sure, what?

BETTY 2
My PUSSY.

BETTY 2
Oh no!

BETTY 2
In a MIRROR.

BETTY 2

Oh my god.

BETTY 2

It was very uncivilised and terrible.

BETTY 2

I can only imagine.

BETTY 2

Let's never speak of it again.

BETTY 2

Let's never.

    Beat.

What did it look like?

BETTY 2
(Getting excited.)

Well.
I wouldn't like to talk about it out loud.
But
I *will* say
that it was very
very

BETTY 2

… Yes??

BETTY 2

Bright.

BETTY 2

Your pussy was…bright?

BETTY 2

Shhh! Not so loud!

BETTY 2

What do you mean 'bright'.

BETTY 2

It was very…vividly…coloured.

BETTY 2
(Driven by curiosity.)
What colour was it? Purple? Gold?

BETTY 2

I don't know the word for that colour.

BETTY 2

You should never go to a dinner party thrown by lesbians, you don't know what might happen!

BETTY 2

I know, it's terrible.

BETTY 2

Do you think they might invite me next time?

BETTY 2

No.

BETTY 2

Why not??

BETTY 2

Because you're just a hand-puppet.

BETTY 2 puts down her hand. She's despondent.

I don't have any friends.
What about…?
No.
What about…?
No.
Or maybe…?
No.

Decisively.

Nope.
I don't have *any* friends.

Beat.

That makes me sad. I feel sad.
I looked at my pussy in a mirror and it was a colour I don't
know how to describe and I don't have any friends and I'm sad.

Beat.

Charles??
Charles!!

Beat.

And Charles isn't home.

> *BETTY 2 picks up a large old school phone receiver. Or makes
> an 'I'm picking up the phone' gesture. She makes a 'phone
> call'. BETTY 3 appears, also 'on the phone'.*

BETTY 2

Hi, is this Betty?

BETTY 3

Yah who is this.

BETTY 2

It's Betty.

BETTY 3

Okay. Whatchou want.

BETTY 2

I guess I wondered if you were at a lesbian party doing lesbian
things?
And if maybe I could come over?

BETTY 3

I went to The Thea-Tah on a date with a married lady and I saw
a famous play inside of another famous play by a dead man
named Rootbeer.

BETTY 2

Oh. You did?

BETTY 3

And I quit my job and *now* I'm a director and an actor and I've decided to put on a play, or actually the best part of that play, which was the littler play, and actually right now I'm casting it.

BETTY 2

Oh. Wow.
I didn't know you liked The Thea-Tah?

BETTY 3

I didn't. Anyway I'm pretty busy, I better go.

BETTY 2

Wait, hold on!

BETTY 3

What.

BETTY 2

I was wondering
if
you were looking for someone else
for your play
if
I could maybe sort of
I don't know
participate…?

BETTY 3

Girl, just because you looked at your pussy in my living room doesn't mean you can participate.

BETTY 2

But I'm bored and lonely and I keep talking to a hand puppet. So can I come over?

BETTY 3

Whaddayou know about The Thea-Tah?

BETTY 2

Well… I don't?

BETTY 3

Hm.

BETTY 2

But! I could be a person who carries things, or a person who moves things, or if there's a person who does voices offstage, I could do that too? And I'll bring rosé!

BETTY 3

You can be my intern.

BETTY 2
(Can't believe her good luck.)

Your intern?

BETTY 3

Unpaid.

BETTY 2

That sounds—wow! That's so great! Thank you!

BETTY 3

And I like whiskey.

BETTY 2

I'll bring you really expensive whiskey.

BETTY 3

See you at rehearsal, intern.

She 'hangs up'.

BETTY 2
(To her hand puppet.)

I have a friend!

8. BETTIES 1 AND 5 DISCUSS TITS AND RAGE

BETTY 5 holds a punching bag.
BETTY 1 punches it. UFC!

BETTY 5

Kill it kill it kill it!

BETTY 1

Die die die!

BETTY 5

KILL IT MORE!

BETTY 1

DIE DIE DIE!

BETTY 5

KILL IT COMPLETELY!

BETTY 1
(In a paroxysm of rage.)
FUCKIN DIE RICHAAAAAAAARDDD!!!

A beat. Oops.

BETTY 5

… Richard?

BETTY 1
(Greatly embarrassed.)
Water. I need water. Can I have water?

BETTY 5 offers her a canteen.

Is that bottled? That isn't bottled.

BETTY 5

It's from the tap.

BETTY 1
(Faintly.)
I don't do tap.

BETTY 5

Here, we do tap.

A beat. BETTY 1 takes the tap water. She makes a face, but she drinks it anyway.

So. Who's Richard?

BETTY 1

Can we not talk about that.

BETTY 5

No, this is good.

BETTY 1

How is this good.

BETTY 5

You suddenly became in touch with the source of your power.

BETTY 1

Richard?

BETTY 5

Wanting to kill Richard.

BETTY 1
(Very hastily.)
I do not want to kill my husband, I love my husband.

A beat—sincere.

You think I'm in touch with the source of my power?

BETTY 5

I think you *were*. Briefly. For a time.

BETTY 1
(Slightly flirtatious.)
What about right now?

BETTY 5

Right now you're sitting down drinking tap water.

Beat.

Tell me about Richard.

BETTY 1

Well.
Richard.
He's very rich.
And very powerful.
And very boring.
And very rich.
And very beige.
And very stumpy.
And very indigestive.
And very alcoholic.
And also still very rich.
That's Richard.

BETTY 5

Okay! Richard!

BETTY 1

And also he's cheating on me.

BETTY 5

With who?

BETTY 1

Someone with very small and perky tits.

BETTY 5

Like yours.

BETTY 1

Mine are not...perky! Are they perky?

BETTY 5

They look perky.

BETTY 1

Thank you.
Wait.
That's none of your—!
Wait.

BETTY 5

If you got a great rack, you got a great rack.
It's like, scientific.
You gonna argue with science?

The energy between them vibrates.

BETTY 1

I guess not.

BETTY 5

Okay then.

Holds up punching bag.

Ready?

BETTY 1

Set.

BETTY 5

Go!

BETTY 1 just fucking kills that punching bag.

BETTY 1

RICHARD
RICHARD
RICCCHAAAAAAARRRRDDDDD!!!

*It's violent and amazing and catastrophic.
And actually super sexy.
BETTY 5 is impressed and attracted.
BETTY 3 comes in.*

BETTY 3

Betty, I heard you were out of prison!

BETTY 5

Hey Betty. Lookin' good.

BETTY 3

         (Fully takes in BETTY 1.)
What's *she* doing here?

Is this a date?

BETTY 5 and 1
(Same time, too fast.)

No!

BETTY 5

—This is a training session!
Betty, this is my client Betty.
Betty, this is my friend Betty.

BETTY 3

I was at your dinner party.

BETTY 1

Oh! That's right.

Really taking her in.

You seem different.

BETTY 3
(Pleased.)

I do?

BETTY 1

Yeah.

BETTY 3

Well, I quit my job, and now I'm kind of a big deal.

BETTY 5

What can I do for you, Betty.

BETTY 3

I stopped by because I've got an opportunity for you. Once in
a lifetime.
Do you want fame? Fortune? Indescribable glory?

BETTY 5

Not really.

BETTY 3

I'm talking about THE THEA-TAH.

BETTY 1
(Immediately interested.)
Oh I love The Thea-Tah, it's so cultural.

BETTY 3
Are white people genetically programmed to say that?

BETTY 5
I don't care about The Thea-Tah. It's for little faggy gay faggy gay boys.

BETTY 3
No, it's for people who wanna be famous and rich! Like me... and you! You see, I am currently Directing and Staging and Inventing a Play. And I have come here to offer you a part in it.

BETTY 1
Ooh, I love plays, I took a class on The Thea-Tah at Amherst.

BETTY 5
You can't invent a play, you don't know any plays.

BETTY 3
I'm inventing a play about the summer, and it's set at midnight, and there is a wall and a lion and everybody dies and it's very sad. And I want you to play the character of The Wall.

BETTY 1
That's *very* cultural. You know, there are people who perform Shakespeare in prisons!

BETTY 5
I worked in the machine shop.

BETTY 1
(Intrigued.)
Oh I didn't know!

BETTY 5
It was awesome, everyone should go.

BETTY 3
(To BETTY 5, impatient.)
All I need is for you to play a Wall! When bitches are cray you make your face blank, and in times of need and crisis you stay solid, like when that pair of tits from New Jersey told me she couldn't date me anymore because she had a boyfriend, and you let me come over and sit in your truck and drunk text her death threats, and all you said was, 'Hope the FBI isn't trackin' that phone' and I don't know anyone else who was born to play a Wall, and I wouldn't ask you if I didn't really need you to be there for me!

BETTY 5
What kinda wall.

BETTY 3
Just a wall. You separate the lovers.

BETTY 5
Who are the lovers?

BETTY 3
Burmese and Frisbee.

BETTY 5
WHO?

BETTY 3
Pyramid and Thirsty?
Penis and Thursday!

BETTY 1
What about me?

BETTY 3
What *about* you?

BETTY 1
Can I have a part?

BETTY 3
Girl. The only part you got is in your hair. And even that shit looks busted.

BETTY 1

My roommate wrote her thesis on Shakespeare and the prison-industrial complex. We were at Amherst!

BETTY 5

Maybe she could be a fence post.

BETTY 3

There aren't any fence posts, there's just a wall.
Are you in or not?

BETTY 5

Fine.

BETTY 3

Fine?

BETTY 5

Fine I'll play a fucking wall.

BETTY 1

And *me*?

BETTY 3

You can be The Moonshine. 'Cause girl, you *white*.

    She leaves.

9. ALL OF THE BETTIES HAVE THEIR FIRST COLLECTIVE EXPERIENCE OF RAGE, ALSO KNOWN AS REHEARSAL

BETTIES 3 and 4.

BETTY 4

What do you mean 'other people'?

BETTY 3

For the play.

BETTY 4

I thought the play was us!

BETTY 3

We need other people, or it isn't a play!

BETTY 4

It could be a play with only two people!

BETTY 3

Nobody likes those.

Beat.

BETTY 4

What other people?

BETTY 3

Just some people. Just other-Betty-with-the-truck-Betty, and skinny white Betty, and my new intern Betty. It's gonna be fine.

BETTY 4

That's a lot of people.

BETTIES 1 and 2 enter, at the same time but they didn't know the other one was coming.

BETTY 1

Oh!

BETTY 2

Oh hi!

BETTY 3

Welcome, everybody, come in!

BETTY 1
(To BETTY 3.)

Hiiiiii!

To BETTY 2.

I didn't know you'd be here.

BETTY 2
(To BETTY 1.)

Betty asked me.

To BETTY 3.

I'm so excited!

BETTY 1

She asked you?

BETTY 2

She especially asked me.
I didn't know *you*'d be here.

BETTY 1

… Betty asked me.
It's very strange that she'd ask *you*.

BETTY 2

Why is that strange?

BETTY 1

Well what was your college major, dear?

BETTY 2

… Canadian Studies?

BETTY 5 enters. She sees BETTY 1 immediately.

BETTY 3 and 4
(To BETTY 5.)

Betty!

BETTY 4

Welcome to our first rehearsal!

BETTY 3

I'm glad you made it!

BETTY 5

(Distracted by BETTY 1.)

Yeah, it's cool.

To BETTY 1.

Hey.

BETTY 1

Oh wow I totally didn't see you, hi.

BETTY 5

Yeah uh. Hi.

BETTY 1

Hi.

The electricity between them sings.
BETTY 1 turns away and fixes her hair.

BETTY 3 doesn't notice, she's really busy being in charge, maybe she's got a clipboard?

BETTY 4

(Sotto, to BETTY 5.)

Are you two...?

BETTY 5

No!

BETTY 4

But...

BETTY 5

No!

BETTY 3

Okay, everybody come to order!

BETTY 4

Everybody listen up!

BETTY 3

Hello Betties!

BETTIES 1, 2, 4 and 5

Hello Betty!

BETTY 3

Today we are gonna have our first rehearsal.
This is the part where I give a speech.
I am so glad to see you all here today.
I saw a play at The Thea-Tah and it was meh, and then Betty

Indicating BETTY 4.

was all, You could do it better, you could be a star,

BETTY 4
(Very pleased to be singled out.)
(Oh, well, I mean…)

BETTY 3

cuz it's like, I got star *quality*, everybody who came to my
counter at Sephora would be like, 'Are you an artist? You did
my face so amazing!'—and if you're an artist the art just breaks
out of you like a fuckin' epidemic all over this shit!

Beat—enough motivational speaking.

Okay now it's time for casting.

BETTY 1

I'm offer-only these days, and she offered me The Moonshine,
so.

BETTY 4

I wanna be an outlaw or a pirate.

BETTY 2

I used to be a model, back when I had an eating disorder, did I
ever tell you that?

BETTY 5

She said I'm a wall.

BETTY 4
(To BETTY 3, super casual.)
Or if you played someone who needed rescuing, I could rescue you.

BETTY 3
Betty!

BETTIES 1, 2, 4 and 5
Yes?

BETTY 3
No, *you* Betty.

To BETTY 1.

You're The Moonshine.

To BETTY 2.

You're The Lion.

To BETTY 4.

You're The Prologue.

To BETTY 5.

You're The Wall.

To ALL.

I'm the director and the writer and the casting director
and I'll be playing the parts of Pyrex and Tambourine.

BETTY 2
(She has never felt so good as she does in this moment.)
Oh wow.
I'm a Lion.
Oh wow.

BETTY 4
What's a Prologue?

BETTY 1
My roommate studied this play in college.

BETTY 5

There was a great gym in prison and I spent a lot of time lifting. I'm gonna rock the shit out of this Wall.

BETTY 5 makes a casual muscle in the direction of BETTY 1, while pretending not to notice her. BETTY 1 totally sees this, but also pretends not to notice.

BETTY 3

Okay, places everybody!

BETTY 4

What's a Prologue, though?

BETTY 1

And where are our scripts?

BETTY 2

I'm a *Lion.*

BETTY 3

This is gonna be a devised piece. I'm devising this.

BETTY 4

What's devised and what's a Prologue?

BETTY 1
(To BETTY 5.)
Devised theatre is so 1970s.

BETTY 5
(Surprised and shy.)
Oh word, that's cool, I wasn't around then.

BETTY 2

Does that mean I can add new bits in?

This stops everybody in their tracks.

BETTY 3

It means *I* can add new bits in.

BETTY 2

But like. If I asked you. And if you said yes. I could add new bits in.

BETTY 3

If you asked me and *if* they were good, which, I mean I can't promise anything, but *if* I said yes, then we could add some bits in.

This opens up the floodgates.

BETTY 1

I want a monologue about boxing!

BETTY 5

I wanna death scene.

BETTY 4

I wanna eat a bat.

BETTY 1
(Stealing looks at BETTY 5.)
I want a death scene too *and* I want a monologue.

BETTY 5
(Stealing looks at BETTY 1.)
I wanna death scene where someone with a monologue shows up.

BETTY 4

I heard Ozzy Osbourne ate a chicken head onstage.

BETTY 1

I want a monologue in which my character ruminates on all the people she's loved and lost, but also the people she's found, maybe by accident, maybe for example at a boxing gym.

BETTY 5 definitely takes this in just as:

BETTY 2
(Timid but with steel.)
I think perhaps I would like to show the audience my pussy.

Everybody looks at BETTY 2.

BETTY 1

That's disgusting.

BETTY 5

That's cool.

BETTY 4

I don't understand The Thea-Tah.

BETTY 3

No no no! We're taking a break. Everybody take ten.

To BETTY 2.

Betty! Get me a latte!
Extra tall skinny carmel splenda non-fat organic double-shot latte.
Thaaaank you!

BETTY 2 goes.

BETTY 4

Did you just send her to get your coffee?

BETTY 3

She's my new intern.
Ay, this is so much harder than I thought it would be.

10. BETTY 4 AND 5 WORK ON THEIR TRUCKS AND TALK ABOUT RELATIONSHIPS, WHICH IS JUST ANOTHER WORD FOR PUSSY.

BETTIES 4 and 5 work on their trucks.

> **BETTY 4**
> *(Meaning BETTY 3.)*

Betty's pretty excited about this Thea-Tah thing.

> **BETTY 5**
> *(Meaning BETTY 1.)*

She's a babe.

> **BETTY 4**
> *('Yeah we know')*

... Ya think?

> **BETTY 5**
> *('Why the attitude?')*

... What.

> **BETTY 4**

Everybody's hot for her.

> **BETTY 5**

... They are?

> **BETTY 4**

You know that!

> **BETTY 5**

I mean. I don't really know her very well.

> **BETTY 4**
> *(Sadly.)*

I feel like nobody knows anybody very well, even if you spent your whole childhood with them and you thought you knew them and you thought maybe you'd invent Thea-Tah together just the two of you but instead they seem more interested in making new friends and having *interns*.

Beat. They work.

BETTY 5

I heard tickets were eighty-five.

BETTY 4

I told you that.

BETTY 5

And like, a million people went.

BETTY 4

Yeah, I told you that.

BETTY 5

A lotta trucks can be purchased with that. A lotta-lotta trucks.

BETTY 4

I know.

BETTY 5

Just for being a Wall.

BETTY 4

Just for being a Prologue.

Beat. They work.

Betty?

BETTY 5

What.

BETTY 4

I'm thinking.

BETTY 5

What-now.

BETTY 4

I looked up a Prologue. And it's just a lotta things you say before things happen.

BETTY 5

Okay.

BETTY 4

I got to thinking about what I might say.
Made me realise, nobody's ever asked me what I have to say.
Especially not *before* something happens.

Beat. They work.

BETTY 5

I don't know that a Wall's gonna have a lot of lines.

BETTY 4

You could maybe add some.
You heard Betty. She said it's devised.

BETTY 5

I don't know.
I've never done that. Like. Made words up.

Beat—meaning BETTY 1.

Betty sounds good no matter what she's saying.

BETTY 4
(Meaning BETTY 3.)

Oh yeah.

BETTY 5

And she got style. Like, not her clothes, but the way she moves.

BETTY 4
(A realisation.)

I guess that's true...

BETTY 5

And she's always surprising me.

BETTY 4

I know. But sometimes it sucks.

BETTY 5

No it doesn't!

BETTY 4

Yeah it does! It used to be good surprises, like 'I'ma skip work and let's go to Coney Island' surprises, and now it's shitty surprises, like 'There's other people in our play' surprises!

BETTY 5

Oh! no no
I mean *Betty.*

BETTY 4

Betty...?

BETTY 5

(Gestures thin, uptight.)

Betty.

BETTY 4

Oh.
OH.
Oh GOD.
That Betty?
You *like* her?

BETTY 5

We been talking about her this whole time!

BETTY 4

(Gestures curvaceous, sexy.)

I thought you meant *Betty!*

BETTY 5

... Ohhhh! NO.

BETTY 4

I knew you were doggin' her!

BETTY 5

No! No.

BETTY 4

And the way she's been looking at *you*—

BETTY 5

No she hasn't!
... Has she?

BETTY 4

Listen.

BETTY 5

What.

BETTY 4

Girls are bad. They're bad for you.
You know?
They can really fuck you up.

BETTY 5

Not if you handle 'em right.
Just gotta get in and get out, you know?
Just can't linger.

BETTY 4

I think they're just not good for you.
I think it's best to avoid.

BETTY 5

I'm just saying. In and out. Don't linger.
Even when you want to.

    Beat. They work.

BETTY 4

I'm gonna come up with a real Prologue.
I got lots to say about what things are and aren't and could be.
I got lots of things I never said.
I'm gonna be the best Prologue Betty ever saw.

BETTY 5

I think maybe The Wall is gonna have a line.

BETTY 4

Yeah?

BETTY 5

Or two. A line or two.

BETTY 4

Yeah that sounds good.

    They work.

11. BETTY 1 HAS MORE RAGE BUT ACTUALLY THIS TIME IT FEELS LIKE A SOLUTION, OR AT THE VERY LEAST, A VALID POINT OF VIEW

BETTY 1

I was watching the News this morning and
there was this series of interviews with Housewives Who Have AIDS
and then I was watching the news and there was a Feature
on Housewives Who Have Cats (With Feline AIDS)
and then I was watching the news and there was a Special Report
on Housewives Whose Husbands All Secretly Have AIDS
and then Richard came home and said You Look Anxious Are You All Right
and I said I Am Going To The Gym, Richard!
and I went to the gym
and instantly I felt better.
And yesterday my cab driver was rude to me, and I said: Take Me To The Gym!
And the day before, the teenage girl at the grocery store judged me with her eyes and I said: Actually I Won't Take Those Salted Caramels, I'm On My Way To The Gym!
And this evening Richard said, I'll Be Coming Home Late Tonight and I said: Well I'll Be Coming Home Late Tonight Too, Actually, Because I Will Be At The Gym!!
I just love hitting things.
I just love it!
I just want to hit everything! With my fists! And with my feet! And with my Eyes! And that is what is going to make me a very good Actor when I play the role of Moonshine, because I will stare at all of the audience members and Hit Them With My Eyes.
Betty is my Boxing Coach, and she is very strange, and very interesting, and also she's a

Whispered.

lesbian

Oh wait—correction.

male-type Gender Lesbian

Correction.

Gender Non Conforming Male-Type Queer... Person

Victorious half beat: she got close!

...and also, she might be the only person on this earth who understands me.

This is real.

And even if she doesn't, I still feel better when she's around.

12. BETTY 3 TELLS US HER THOUGHTS
AND FEELINGS, BECAUSE WE CARE,
BECAUSE SHE IS GOING TO BE ALL THE RAGE

*BETTY 3 faces us. BETTY 2 watches her hungrily. We are her adoring
audience. With a big smile.*

BETTY 3

Sooo today's MONDAY and
my personal assistant got me coffee and
I'm thinking about the latest brand I'm going to launch
called STAR
for stars
(it might be a perfume or a maxi-pad)
and
I'm working on my latest project
which is a Play
in The Thea-Tah
and I'm directing it and starring in it
and I just think it says a lot about community
and diversity and respect
and homelessness in children
and Israel and Palestine, but not overtly
and also it's a love story
and love is very important
because a lot of people don't feel loved
and then they do things like join gangs and kill people
and do drugs and become investment bankers.
When I was younger nobody valued me
so I didn't value myself
so I went on lots of dates with bitches who didn't deserve my time
like that puta from Long Island who gave me a rash
and then one day I looked in the mirror
and I was like, GIRL. YOU ARE HOT.
YOU ARE FIERCE.
YOU ARE A FIERCE MOTHERFUCKER.
YOU ARE THE VOICE OF YOUR GENERATION.
And then I became those things.
And I stopped dating.
And I feel good!

I'm a rebel.
I don't give a fuck.
YOLO!

She signs off.

BETTY 2

I wish I was like you.

BETTY 3

There can only be one me.
And I'm it.

BETTY 2

I don't like myself very much.

BETTY 3
(Not meanly.)
I can see why. I don't mean that in a bad way.

BETTY 2

Maybe I can be different, not exactly like you, but sort of like
you, but different in a way that then becomes different like me.

BETTY 3

You're overthinking this.

BETTY 2

My mother taught me never to raise my voice or look upset or
ruin my make-up in public and also not in private either. So I'm
not going to cry. But I feel like I could.

BETTY 3

Okay. Look.
Here's what you gotta do.
You gotta think about who you wanna be.
And then become her.

A real beat.

BETTY 2

Well. I don't know that many people.
I know my husband Charles. And I guess you.
And I know Betty.
And I guess I also know Betty and Betty.

BETTY 3

Okay, so that's like, five different people that you know.

BETTY 2

I don't want to be like Betty and Betty.

Meaning BETTY 1.

Or like Betty.

BETTY 3

If you're saying that you're in love with me, everybody's in love
with me, now that I'm famous. So that's just like, something
that happens.

BETTY 2

No I think I'm saying that I want everybody to be in love with me?
Except maybe what I'm saying is that I want to be in love with
myself?
I looked at my pussy last night—

BETTY 3

Girl, you got to stop with that—

BETTY 2

—after rehearsal—

BETTY 3

—that was a one-time activity!

BETTY 2

—and I thought I'd never seen anything more *interesting*.

BETTY 3

Your specific pussy?

BETTY 2

I've never seen a different one.
Do you want to show me yours?

BETTY 3

No I do not want to show you my pussy!

BETTY 2

Why not?

BETTY 3

Because I am a grown-ass woman who is an artist and an innovator and an entrepreneur and I define myself by more than my pussy, even though it is important for me to know WHAT and WHERE my pussy is, and how to use it, when I feel like using it!

BETTY 2

I don't think anything is more interesting than my specific pussy, including all the ways in which I've been defined up until now.

BETTY 3

I gotta go.

She turns to go.

BETTY 2

See you at rehearsal!

13. BETTY 2 WATCHES HER PUSSY INSTEAD OF A DOCUMENTARY ABOUT LIONS, AND THEN SHARES SOMETHING PROFOUND WITH US

BETTY 2

Sooo…today's Monday
and
I am Betty's personal assistant
for the duration of her current theatrical production
and
also I play the lead
specifically speaking, a Lion.
And I have never played a Lion before, so I'm not sure where
to start
except with research, lots of research
so last night I sat down to watch all of David Attenborough's
videos about the Serengeti
and Africa
and Lions
Great Cats of all kinds
and instead while the movie was playing
I put my hand-mirror down
down there
and I just
looked
at that
instead.
For the entire documentary.
And then it ended and I started it back at the beginning
so that I wouldn't have missed it
and then somehow instead I just
kept
looking
down there.
So.
I watched my pussy for two hours and seventy-five minutes
which is the duration of the documentary times three
and then Charles came home from work.

And Charles said: Betty, it's late, why are you still up. Let's go to bed.
And I said: Charles, I was at rehearsal, I'm in a play, and I'm doing homework.
And Charles said: That's nice. I like movies better.
And then he fell asleep.
And then I lay awake.
All night.
Me and my pussy together.

Beat. A deep breath.

And then I wrote an erotic story.
I wrote it in my head first
for a long time
and then somewhere around 3am
I got up and I wrote it on paper
and then it was still happening inside me so
I started reading it out loud
I was reading it and reading it and
Charles woke up and said: Are you talking in your sleep
and I said: I am reading an erotic story I wrote, Charles
and Charles said: It's a little late, Betty,
and then he went back to sleep.
And here is my erotic story.

BETTY 2 recites her erotic story:

This is an erotic story about a lion.
It takes its lion cock and puts it in things
like dust bowls and small holes and ant hills.
Its lion cock is like a handgun or a drill or a Swiss Army Knife because it's all-purpose.
This is also a story about the lions who don't have sex.
They are constantly waiting for rain, and their ribs show.
They are the kinds of lions who go looking for discounts in places where there are no good discounts. They are the lions who clip coupons but then leave the coupons at home.
They are the lions who believe the late night infomercials, and they are the lions who leave the TV on so they don't feel alone,

and they are the lions who look at themselves in the mirror and say: ugly ugly lion, and they are the lions who are afraid of themselves, and they are the lions who wake up one day and say: I FUCKING HATE ALL OF THIS, and they are the lions who will someday star in a play.
This is a story about all of the lions.

A long deep breath.

I hate all of this, Charles. And I'm starring in a play.

14. THE BETTIES BRING THEIR DEVISED PIECES TO REHEARSAL; THE WALL HAS LINES

BETTIES 1 and 5 get to rehearsal early, at the same time.

BETTY 5

Oh hey.

BETTY 1

Oh! hey!

BETTY 5

Hey.

BETTY 1

Hey.

> *An awkward moment. They look at each other while trying not to look at each other.*

BETTY 5

Hey, next time you come down to the gym, I got a new punching bag.

> *Now they're on comfortable ground! The energy between them is suddenly easy and electric again.*

BETTY 1

You did?

BETTY 5

Yeah, now that you're hitting harder, figured it was time for a heavier one.

BETTY 1

Am I? Hitting harder. Than I was.

BETTY 5

Oh! Yeah. Yeah you definitely are.

> *BETTY 1 smiles at BETTY 5. It's so genuine that it sort of takes BETTY 5's breath away.*

BETTY 1

Betty…

But before she can say whatever she's going to say, BETTY 4 enters.

BETTY 4
(To BETTY 5.)

Hey Betty.

To BETTY 1, a nod.

Betty.

BETTY 1 and 5
(Super casual, turning their backs on each other.)

Oh hey Betty.

BETTY 3 enters, clipboard in hand, BETTY 2 behind her, carrying pencils.

BETTY 3

Good morning Betties!

BETTIES 1, 2, 4 and 5

Good morning Betty!

BETTY 3

Everybody come to order!

BETTY 4
(To BETTY 3.)

Betty, can we talk for a sec?

BETTY 3

Rehearsal is starting.

BETTY 4

Yeah but I was just thinking…maybe we could talk about what we're gonna do in rehearsal today.

BETTY 3

I made a plan.

BETTY 4

You did?

BETTY 3

Yeah, you can't be the director and the lead and the casting director and not have a plan.

BETTY 4

Well… I mean yeah, no…but I guess I sort of thought maybe we could do that together.

BETTY 3

It would've taken longer if we did it together, Betty.
OK, everybody get in place!
We are going to play zip zap zop.

BETTY 1

Oh I love this game!

BETTY 3
(To BETTY 1.)

Zip!

BETTY 1
(To BETTY 2.)

Zap!

BETTY 2
(To BETTY 5.)

Zop!

BETTY 5
(To BETTY 3.)

Zip!

BETTY 3
(To BETTY 4.)

Zap!

BETTY 4

… What.

BETTY 3
(Prompting her.)

Zop!

BETTY 4

I don't know what you want me to do.

BETTY 3
(Does the gesture.)
Just fucking Zop somebody, Betty!

BETTY 4

This is why nobody goes to The Thea-Tah.

BETTY 3
(Consulting her clipboard again.)
You know what, nevermind.

BETTY 5
(Aside, to BETTY 4.)
Are you OK?

BETTY 3

Okay, now I want everybody to pick a partner.

BETTIES 1, 2, 4 and 5
(Together.)
I pick Betty.

A beat, they're all confused.

BETTY 5
(To BETTY 1.)
You wanna?

BETTY 1 does.

BETTY 4
(To BETTY 3.)
You Betty.

BETTY 2
(Soft.)
Nobody picked me.

BETTY 3

(Taking BETTY 4's hands.)

Now I want you all to take your partner's hands in your hands and look them in the eyes and you're gonna mirror back to them things you notice about them.

This is almost physically painful for BETTY 4.

You have tattoos.

BETTY 4

Your hair is getting long.

BETTY 3

Yes! Yours is getting short!

BETTY 5 takes BETTY 1's hands. This physical contact makes them both awkward and also kind of wired.

BETTY 1

My hands are kind of sweaty.

BETTY 5

Nah, they're perfect. I mean. Dry, they're dry.

BETTY 1

My college roommate and I used to do this.

BETTY 5

You did?

BETTY 1

(Giggling.)

Yeah and then we made out.

BETTY 5

… You *did*?

BETTY 3

Things you notice, everybody. Look at your partner and tell them what you *notice*.

BETTY 4

(To BETTY 3.)

Everything, actually.

BETTY 3 doesn't hear this—she's looking around to make sure that BETTIES 1 and 5 are doing it correctly.

BETTY 2
(Very sad and soft.)

Who's my partner?

BETTY 1

Okay tell me the things you notice about me.

BETTY 5

Uh.
Well…
You got new earrings.

BETTY 1

My husband Richard got them for me this morning, I told him:
I know you're cheating, Richard, and then he brought me
earrings. If you asked Richard what he noticed about me,
he wouldn't even see me. He'd look right at me and say
Where'd she go?

BETTY 5

You got a new muscle.

BETTY 1
(Totally off-balanced.)

—What?

BETTY 5

A new muscle. Right there.
From punching things.

BETTY 1 looks. She's right.

BETTY 1

Oh my god.
I have a new muscle!

They grin at each other, both inordinately delighted.

BETTY 5

You have a new muscle!

BETTY 1

I have a new muscle!

BETTY 1 hugs BETTY 5 impulsively, very tightly. BETTY 5 lets herself be hugged, and feels herself become a maelstrom of confusion and longing. Meanwhile:

BETTY 4

I texted you a picture of my truck last night but I *noticed* that you didn't text me back, did you not, like, see it or something?

BETTY 3

Betty! You have to tell me things you notice about *me*.

BETTY 4

I notice that I haven't seen you around much. At all. These days. Are you going on a lot of dates?

BETTY 3

I don't have time to do anything other than develop my brand. And you're not doing this exercise right.

BETTY 4

So...you're not dating *at all*, or like...?

BETTY 3

The whole point of this exercise is to be observational.
You can't ask questions, you gotta observe! You gotta be very specific about what and how you observe, because everything you do shapes the performer you're going to be. I read this personality profile about a very famous actress who played this chick Paraphernalia and she did her kegels every time she was onstage as Paraphernalia and everybody knew there was something very different and very special about her performance but nobody knew what it was. And it was her kegels. Everything counts.

BETTY 2

I don't have a partner.
I am The Lion in the endless line of sexless lions.
I am The Lion in the part of the Serengeti where it never rains.

BETTY 5
(A burst of impulse.)
Maybe we could go out sometime.

BETTY 1
Excuse me?

BETTY 5
I said maybe we could work out sometime. Together.

BETTY 1
We're already working out together.

BETTY 5
Yeah no I know.

BETTY 3
Okay everybody! Shake it out!
Let's just start at the beginning and work through and get a
general shape for all of this.

To BETTY 4.

Betty, would you like to share with us where you are in your
process as The Prologue?

BETTY 4
(Delighted to be picked, but on the spot.)
Where I am?

BETTY 3
Yeah, where you are. Where your instincts are leading you.

BETTY 4
Oh!
Well.
Yeah.
So…

BETTY 3
I'll set the scene for all of us. It's a dark night. And here's The Wall.

Arranges BETTY 5.

And The Moonshine is shining.

Arranges BETTY 1.

And The Prologue walks out.

Arranges BETTY 4.

And introduces the whole situation.

BETTY 4

Well.
Uh.

BETTY 3

Go on.

BETTY 4

Um.

BETTY 3

You got this!

BETTY 4

Well…

BETTY 5

I got something.

BETTY 4

You're The Wall.

BETTY 5

Yeah but I got an idea.

BETTY 3

This is the part where The Prologue happens.

BETTY 4

Yeah she called on me.

BETTY 5

Yeah but The Wall is onstage first. So maybe actually The Wall
should talk first.

BETTY 4

She picked me.

BETTY 3

What's your idea?

BETTY 4

For *real*?

BETTY 5

I'm a wall called The Wall.
Richard The Wall.

BETTY 1

Richard?

BETTY 3

There's nobody in this play called Richard...

BETTY 5

I stand here. Day after day.
You think I don't hear you.
I hear you.
You think I don't see you.
I see you.
You think you're alone in a room.
But there's walls. Four walls.
I'm one of them.
You might think all Walls are the same.
I could be a different Wall for you.
I could be a different Richard.

BETTY 3

I don't understand any of this.

BETTY 4

Oh hold up.

BETTY 5

I never met anybody I wanted to be a different Wall for.
But if you live in a house that doesn't appreciate you.
I wanna be the house that does.

Beat.

That's it. That's the lines I got.
Now maybe The Prologue can talk.

BETTY 1, deeply moved, begins to clap.

BETTY 4

This is bullshit. I quit.

BETTY 3

What? Wait!!

BETTY 4 walks out. BETTY 3 runs after her.

BETTY 2

I never had a partner.
And we never got to The Lion.
But I guess rehearsal is over?
So I guess I'll go home now.

She leaves. Beat.

BETTY 1

You should come over for dinner sometime.

BETTY 5

Dinner?

BETTY 1

Sure. Just whenever. Just no big deal. I'll just whip up something casual. Or we could order pizza.

BETTY 5

To your house?

BETTY 1

Girl's Night In.

BETTY 5

Yeah maybe.

BETTY 1

Slumber Party. Whatever.

BETTY 5

Slumber Party?

BETTY 1

Whatever.

BETTY 5

I guess that sounds fun.

BETTY 1

Great! I'll check my schedule. I'm *very very* busy but actually I might have a *small* window of time sometime like...tonight.

BETTY 5

I'll be there.

15. BETTY 4 HAS RAGE, BUT IT'S THE KIND OF RAGE WHERE YOU LOVE THE PERSON YOU'RE ANGRY AT, SO YOU JUST FEEL SICK AND A LITTLE CRAZY, WHICH MAY BE WHY SHE AUDITIONS FOR THE PART OF THE WALL

BETTIES 3 and 4.

BETTY 3

Hold up! Wait!

BETTY 4

I'm done waiting.

BETTY 3

Why are you so mad?

BETTY 4

Because the system is fucked. And you lied to me!

BETTY 3

I never lied to you, how did I lie to you.

BETTY 4

I thought we were in this together! And now it's a lot of other people and you're giving them all special treatment!

BETTY 3

I'm not giving anybody anything other than the disdain I reserve for everybody!

BETTY 4

You never used to talk like that.
You never used to use words like 'disdain'.
And now you're hanging out with Betty and Betty and their fucking Upper East Side manicures and their sad shriveled pussies that they look at in *your* hand-mirror and that is fucked up! It used to be me and you!

BETTY 3

And other-Betty-with-the-truck-Betty.

BETTY 4

And other-Betty-with-the-truck-Betty! But now she only ever
wants to talk about Prison, and I never even went to Prison,
and you don't have time for me anymore!

BETTY 3

Listen.
Betty.
I hear you.
I hear what you're going through.
But I also need you to hear what I'm going through.

BETTY 4

Which is what!

BETTY 3

It is *hard* to be a playwright-director-actor-activist-celebrity!
Everybody always needs to know what I am thinking and
feeling, and I always need to be thinking about the orphans
and the hanta virus and the dying rainforests, because I have
become the voice of a generation and my generation has a lot
to say, even if we don't spell very well.

    Beat—calling:

Betty!
Where's my latte!!

    Beat—with gravitas and tragedy.

And now my assistant is missing.

BETTY 4

Look.
Other Betty with the truck is just in rehearsal to pick up skinny
white Betty. And she's not taking The Wall seriously as a
character. And I know I kinda froze up as The Prologue today,
but maybe that's because actually I'm a better Wall. Because
Walls just stand still while everything around them changes, and
they can't do anything, and they can't say anything, and nobody
knows how they feel, and these days, all I feel like is… A Wall.

    BETTY 3 feels guilty and conflicted.

BETTY 3

Betty, I don't know what to tell you! I'm responsible for a lot of moving parts right now and I'm overwhelmed! I don't even sleep anymore, I just lie awake at night and make lists of things I need to accomplish, and my heart races. This is more stressful than Sephora!

BETTY 4

Look, I'm just saying maybe I should be The Wall. That's all I'm saying.

BETTY 3

I cast you because I thought you were the best one for the part of The Prologue! I don't know how you are for The Wall! I haven't auditioned you for The Wall! I made a direct offer for The Prologue! And you couldn't even do The Prologue! I need advil. I need a vacation.

BETTY 4

Well what if I auditioned for you right now for the role of The Wall.

BETTY 3

I'm understaffed.

BETTY 4

What if I did a very very very short audition for The Wall. And then I could get you a latte.

A beat. BETTY 3 considers her options.

BETTY 3

Extra-skinny low-fat high-fructose gluten-free soy-rice organic with a dash of cinnamon?

BETTY 4

You used to get coffee at Dunkin' Donuts.

BETTY 3

… Excuse me?

BETTY 4

We used to be friends and you used to get coffees from Dunkin' Donuts. And now I never see you and you drink things that are hard to remember.

BETTY 3

It's called progress. I'm progressing.

BETTY 4

Oh.

A beat. BETTY 3 takes pity.

BETTY 3

Okay fine. I will audition you—*very very* briefly—for the role of The Wall. After which I'll write down my order for you so you don't forget it.

BETTY 4

Thank you! Okay. I'm just going to do a few different Walls for you, very quickly.
This is my Wall Number One: A Brick Wall.

She stands very still: intense and expressionless.

This is my Wall Number Two: A Plaster Wall.

Same thing.

This is my Wall Number Three: A Straw Wall.

She gives the same intense, expressionless Wall Three.

BETTY 3

Well! Okay.
Thank you very much.

BETTY 4

You're welcome. Am I hired?

BETTY 3

I'll call you back about that.

BETTY 4

When?

BETTY 3

Later.

BETTY 4

Later when? I don't wanna be pushy I just need to know because
of my schedule, because of what days I'm gonna be working
on my truck and what days I'm gonna be a Wall, those are just
things I'd need to work out ahead of time.

A moment. And then:

BETTY 3

I think maybe you should still be The Prologue.

A beat.

BETTY 4
(Defeated.)

Oh.

Pause.

I'ma get you a coffee now.
But I'm going to Dunkin' Donuts.

She leaves.

16. BETTIES 1 AND 5 HAVE A SLUMBER PARTY

BETTIES 1 and 5 are SO awkward. BETTY 5 likes BETTY 1 so much that she's lost her game. And BETTY 1 never had any to start with.

BETTY 5

Uh. So
What
do you
generally
do
at a slumber party?

BETTY 1

Well!
We could paint our toenails?

BETTY 5

Hm...

BETTY 1

Or we could do each other's make-up!

BETTY 5

Mmm...

BETTY 1

We could do each other's hair?

BETTY 5

Well...

BETTY 1

(Crushed.)
I haven't had a slumber party since college.
You're having a terrible time. I'm a terrible host.

BETTY 5

No! No. I'm having a great time.

BETTY 1

No you're not.

BETTY 5

I mean. I've never been to a slumber party?
So I'm maybe doing things wrong.

BETTY 1

You've *never* slept over with a girl?

BETTY 5

I mean...that's a little different.

A beat between them—electricity.

Maybe I should go home?

BETTY 1

I want you to stay.

BETTY 5

Even if I'm a bad slumber party guest?

BETTY 1

Well I'm a bad slumber party host, so.

It heats up.

BETTY 5

What other kinds of things did you do at slumber parties?

BETTY 1

We talked about boys. Mostly.

BETTY 5

Oh.

BETTY 1

And we made out with each other.

BETTY 5
(More interest.)

Oh!

BETTY 1

And also we cried.

BETTY 5

Did you cry about Richard?

BETTY 1

I didn't cry about Richard because I didn't know Richard.
I didn't meet Richard until after college, when I had to get married.
College was about slumber parties and boys and crying, not
about Richard.

BETTY 5

Do you cry about Richard now?

A beat.

BETTY 1

Not anymore.

Beat.

Do you have. Like. A person?

BETTY 5

A person...

BETTY 1

A Lesbian Girlfriend Person?

BETTY 5

No.

BETTY 1

Or like a Gender Queer Girlfriend Person?

BETTY 5

I can't say that I do right now, no.

BETTY 1

Or like a person who doesn't always know what those words
mean but is learning even when she gets it wrong, type person?

BETTY 5

I didn't used to want any kind of person.
But I don't feel like that anymore.

A beat between them.

BETTY 1

And we played dress up.

BETTY 5

How come?

BETTY 1

I don't know, we just did.

BETTY 5

I don't think I'd fit in your clothes.

BETTY 1

No I guess not.

BETTY 5

I bet I'd fit in Richard's.

A beat.

BETTY 1

You think?

BETTY 5

Yeah.

BETTY 1

Let's see.

A beat. BETTY 1 gets an armload of Richard's clothing.

BETTY 5

For real?

BETTY 1

Try them on!

BETTY 5

Don't look.

She starts to change—flirting.

You're looking.

BETTY 1
(Flirting.)

No I'm not.

BETTY 5

(As she changes.)

I been thinking a lot about being a Wall.

About how I know a lot more than I thought I knew about being a Wall.

Cuz I kinda go through life like a Wall.

A lot of times when I'm walking down the street and asshole guys yell shit at me?

I pretend my face is a Wall.

Or when other Betty-with-the-truck-Betty is sad and I don't know what to say.

Or when my best friend in Prison was like, I can't be your best friend, and I was like, why not, and she was like, you fingered me in the showers, and I was like, you wanted me to! And she was like, yeah I thought I wanted to but afterwards I wished I hadn't and now we can't be best friends.

I pretended I was a Wall that time too.

And I think maybe I'm actually really really good at being a Wall, and Walls are things that people lean against, so maybe that's a good thing. And I don't think I ever woulda realised that if I wasn't in a Play in The Thea-Tah where I had to be a Wall. So maybe The Thea-Tah isn't for faggy gay pansy-boys after all. But maybe it still is. I haven't made up my mind about that entirely.

You can look now.

How do I look?

BETTY 1 turns around.

BETTY 5 is in Richard Drag. It looks good. A beat between them.

BETTY 1

You look good.

Beat.

Now what?

BETTY 5

Now you do it.

17. BETTY 2 CURATES THE ENVIRONMENT IN WHICH SHE IS MOST LIKELY TO FLOURISH

BETTY 2 with her hand puppet.

BETTY 2

And then we were supposed to pick a partner but nobody picked me.

BETTY 2

That sucks.

BETTY 2

And then everybody talked to each other but not to me.

BETTY 2

Oh no.

BETTY 2

And I just stood very very still and waited to disappear.

BETTY 2

Oh god.

BETTY 2

And then I came home and Charles was still at work and I lay on his side of the bed and smelled his side of the pillow but I didn't feel comforted at all, I just felt like I was lying on a stranger's side of the bed and smelling a stranger's pillow.

BETTY 2

Your life is bleak and dismal. Maybe you should drink a lot of pills.

BETTY 2

Oh! Do you think so?

BETTY 2

Yeah maybe.

BETTY 2

I'm not sure that's the solution.

BETTY 2

Maybe you should drink a lot of pills with a handle of whiskey, and then drive your car into a lake.

BETTY 2

I don't really know where the nearest lake is.

BETTY 2

There's maps.

BETTY 2

That's true.

BETTY 2

You could look at a map.

BETTY 2

I guess I could.

BETTY 2

I think you should take a lot of pills and drink a handle of whiskey and look at a map and then drive your car into the nearest lake. I think that's probably the best thing to do.

BETTY 2

I mean. Don't you think? That might be...?

BETTY 2

What.

BETTY 2

A little...drastic?

BETTY 2

What. So what. Drastic is good. Drastic is better than dismal.

BETTY 2

But I just mean: Things Get Better.

BETTY 2

What?? No they don't!

BETTY 2

They don't?

BETTY 2

That's the biggest pile of steaming bullshit.
That's the biggest rankest most putrid diarrhea-pit of bullshit.
Things Never Get Better!!

BETTY 2

They *don't?*

BETTY 2

No! It's scientifically proven! They just get worse and worse and worse and then they're over. The only real way to take charge of any given situation of bleak dismal awfulness is to end it before it ends on its own.

BETTY 2

Oh.

BETTY 2

I can't believe you didn't already know that.

BETTY 2

No. Maybe I knew that.

    A beat.

BETTY 2

So...what are you gonna do?

BETTY 2

I'm gonna throw a dinner party.

BETTY 2

A *dinner* party?

BETTY 2

Yes!
A dinner party that is also a dress rehearsal
that is also a revolution
that is also a re-boot
And you're not invited.

BETTY 2

Then who's gonna help you throw the dinner party?

BETTY 2

A Lion.

18. BETTY 2, HAVING COME TO THE END OF HER ABILITY TO BE A BETTY, BECOMES A LION AND THROWS A DINNER PARTY, THAT IS ALSO A DRESS REHEARSAL, THAT IS ALSO A POINT OF NO RETURN

BETTY 2 takes off all necklaces/jewellery/earrings. She strips away. She does not add anything on.

This moment is efficient and purposeful. Suddenly! The whole world transforms! This might be a breaking apart of some kind, a re-shaping. It is instantaneous and elaborate, and it fills the space with colour and life, unlike the stripped down state we've existed in so far.

There are so many balloons and streamers. Maybe there are inflatables? Who knows! There is a make-your-own sundae station—a giant amount of ice cream (that will melt throughout, and that may or may not be in a bathtub or a kiddie pool), fistfuls of coloured sprinkles, M&Ms, gummy bears, etc. No other types of food or drink. It is like a particularly strange child's birthday party meets a reckless-outlaw-party-on-steroids.

BETTY 2 takes a deep breath. Here we go! The other BETTIES pour in from different directions.

BETTIES 1 and 5 are dressed as Richard.
BETTY 3 is dressed Ultra Glam.
BETTY 4 is like she always is. She's come from working on her truck.

BETTIES 1, 3, 4 and 5
(To BETTY 2, and each other.)

Betty!
Hey Betty.
Betty, so good to see you!

BETTY 3
(To BETTY 2.)
I love what you've done with the space, Betty.

BETTY 4
(To BETTY 5.)
Whoa Betty, new look.

BETTY 5

Actually, it's Richard.

BETTY 1

And Richard for me too, please.

BETTY 4

... What?

BETTY 2

Thanks for coming, Richards!
I was planning my dinner party and then I realised that I hate dinner and I love ice cream, so the ice cream station is over there and you can make your own sundaes.

Already attacking the ice cream station:

BETTY 5

Awesome.

BETTY 1

Ooh look at that.

BETTY 3

Thanks for having us, Betty!

BETTY 2

You're welcome, and actually
I'm a Lion.

BETTY 4

Wait what?

BETTY 2

Betty couldn't make it tonight, so I'm throwing this party for her and I'm a Lion
and Lions particularly appreciate ice cream because in the desert there so rarely is any.

BETTY 3
(Taking all of this in.)

... Huh.

BETTY 1

Cool, nice to meet you.

BETTY 5

What's up, Lion.

Maybe a sticky fist bump.

BETTY 4

I don't understand anything.

BETTY 3 decides it's time to get this back on track.

BETTY 3

Okay *well*! it's very nice of Bet—of The Lion to host us for our final-dinner-dress-party-rehearsal, because tomorrow is our opening-night-first-performance and The Press will be coming!

BETTIES 1, 3, 4 and 5

The Press??

BETTY 3

The Press! So I want us all to assemble for a run-through. Richards! Lion! Betty! We are going to walk through the show from the top.

BETTY 4

(To BETTY 3.)

—*You're* still Betty right?

BETTY 3

I'm Betty & Fabulous.

As everybody gathers, increasingly sticky but game.

All right everyone! I'll set the scene for all of us. It's a dark night. And The Wall—

Wait a minute.

… Where is The Wall?

All the BETTIES look around at each other.

BETTY 2

I don't think we have a Wall anymore.

BETTY 3

OK then The Moonshine Enters!

BETTY 5

We don't have Moonshine either.

BETTY 1

We just have Richards.

BETTY 3

This is a disaster.

BETTY 2

I think The Richards should enter.

They all look at her.

It is a dark night...and here are The Richards.

BETTIES 1 and 5 step forward. There is a real joy and electricity about all of this—they are creating, and they're doing it together.

BETTY 1

Richard!

BETTY 5

Yes Richard?

BETTY 1

I often think about Finance and The Automotive Industry.

BETTY 5

Richard, I myself, I confess, often think about Gambling and Drinking and Vice.

BETTY 1

Richard, that's very lascivious and exciting!

BETTY 5

Oh, Richard, do you think so? Thank you very much, old chap.

BETTY 1

Richard, you are almost a Brother to me.

BETTY 5

Richard, I so enjoy our Hunting and Fishing Trips, and the Time we spend Alone...

Has an epiphany.

... In The Same Tent!

The air sizzles.

BETTY 3

Okay! Very good! and then—stand by, Richards—The Prologue Enters.

BETTY 4 walks 'onstage'.

And The Prologue addresses the Audience.

BETTY 4 is silent.

The Prologue speaks!

BETTY 4 is silent.

Betty! The Prologue!

BETTY 4 is silent.

We talked about this!

BETTY 2

I have something.

BETTY 3

You're The Lion!

BETTY 2

I know! And The Lion walks onstage.

Walks 'onstage'.

And The Lion sees the Richards, and The Lion sees The Prologue and The Lion sees Pyramus and Thisbe and the Director and the Casting Director who are all played by Betty (hello Betty), and The Lion says:
I am so happy to be here.

BETTY 1

Oh that's nice.

BETTY 5

I like that.

BETTY 2

The Lion says: I would like to give a toast.

BETTY 3

… A toast?

BETTY 2

I want to give a toast to friends and to lesbians and to Betties who perform in The Thea-Tah and to Betty Who Could Not Be Here Tonight But In Whose Honor I Am Throwing This Dinner Party. You see, Betty is the epitome of perfection. Betty is the love of my life and a crystalline example of devotion. Betty is a rock and I am a limpet of adoration. I want to live underneath her ribs so I can hug her heart all the time. That's just how I feel about Betty. To Betty!

The BETTIES are sold. Even BETTY 4.

BETTIES 1, 3, 4 and 5

Cheers To Betty!

BETTY 3

Okay! Yes! The Lion gives a toast, and then The Prologue says…

BETTY 4

… You're not gonna like it.

BETTY 3

I'm gonna love it! Just say something!

BETTY 4

… I really don't think you will.

The Richards intercede.

BETTY 5

I think the Richards have another scene.

BETTY 1

Yeah, I think Richard says something like:
I like your Tie, Richard old buddy.

BETTY 5

And Richard might say:
I like *your* Cuff-Links, Richard old man.

BETTY 1

I like your Jaw Line, Richard old chap.

BETTY 5

I confess I find your Shoulders astonishing.

BETTY 1

(Her Richard voice falls away throughout.)
However, Richard, I have a thought.

BETTY 5

What's that, Richard?

BETTY 1

Or perhaps it's more of an observation.

BETTY 5

Go on, Richard old chap, please.

BETTY 1

You have an…eyelash.

BETTY 5

An eyelash?

BETTY 1

Right there.

ETTY 5

Right where?

BETTY 1

Come here, Richard.

> BETTY 5 comes close.
> BETTY 1 kisses her.
> They make out, as Richards.
> But also, they make out.

BETTY 2
(Entranced.)

Oh wow!

BETTY 4
(Kind of amazed.)

Oh shit.

BETTY 3
(This is finally going well!)

Oh that was a surprise!

BETTY 2
(As The Lion, whipped up.)

I also want to talk about Betty's pussy! It's a perfect object.
Like a small clock or a marzipan fruit or something very precise
and unusual and unreplicable. It could be in a museum. In a
box or on a shelf or behind glass or none of those things at all,
maybe on a tall post so it could be viewed without some kind
of barrier separating it from the audience. Betty's pussy is an
artifact of perfection. To Betty!

BETTY 3 and 4

To Betty!!

BETTY 1 and 5
(Break apart to say.)

Yeah Betty!!!

BETTY 5

You good?

BETTY 1

Let's go.

BETTY 3

Wait—the show isn't over!

BETTY 1 and 5

Bye guys!

BETTIES 1 and 5 exit. BETTY 3 grasps at straws, trying to make the best of this.

BETTY 3

The Richards exit! And The Prologue speaks!

BETTY 4

Betty...

BETTY 3

You have to speak, I can't enter until you speak!

BETTY 4

Betty...

BETTY 3

Say something!!

BETTY 4 hesitates, struggling with the thing she needs to say.

BETTY 2
(This is for herself, not even for them.)
More than a toast, I want to say to Betty and her pussy: Charles went to bed when you and your pussy were awake. Charles never understood the importance of the Serengeti until you and your pussy, and he still may not. Charles is a sad sad man. He doesn't know that happiness is an important thing. And I'm sorry for that, and I'm sorry that he never told you that happiness was important, and I'm sorry that your pussy had to be the one to tell you that. But I'm glad somebody did. To Betty's pussy!

BETTIES 3 and 4 don't clock this, and BETTY 2 doesn't need them to. BETTY 2 toasts herself and drinks, a long and thoughtful drink. She is dizzy with liberation. BETTY 4 takes a deep breath and makes a decision.

BETTY 4

OK. But I warned you.
'This sucks and we should both quit.'

BETTY 3

... What?

BETTY 4

'You used to be my best friend, and I had a crush on you,
but now it's more of a hate-crush.'

BETTY 3

A hate-crush??

BETTY 4

'And I wish we never invented The Thea-Tah at all. So let's quit.'

BETTY 3

We can't quit!!

BETTY 4

(Really asking.)

Why not?

BETTY 3

Because everybody has to know who I am!
Everybody has to listen when I talk!
I want everybody to love me, even if we've never met!
Maybe after I get all those things I can quit, but that's gonna
take a while.

This comes from the depths of BETTY 4's soul.

BETTY 4

Betty... *I* know who you are, and *I* listen when you talk
and I think you're pretty, and I think you're smart
and the thing is:
everybody loving you is actually the same thing as nobody
loving you.
So if you wanna make Thea-Tah, you can make Thea-Tah
and if you wanna change, I guess that's okay too
But you should know that *I* love you—even when I hate-crush
you—

---

and you don't have to love me back in the same way
but I think you should come for a ride in my truck.
And this is the thing that I want to say to you, before
everything else happens,
which, I guess, makes this my Prologue
(and I would never have had a Prologue if it weren't for you
and The Thea-Tah so I guess I've changed too)
(and that isn't as bad as I thought it would be, so thank you for that)
but also: The Thea-Tah is breaking my heart.

A beat. BETTY 3 is moved by this in ways she didn't know she could be.

BETTY 3

Okay.

BETTY 4

Okay...?

BETTY 3

Yeah, okay.
I'll come for a ride.

BETTY 4

You will?

BETTY 3

Yeah.

BETTY 4

... Oh.

BETTY 3
(A little shy.)

You did good.

BETTY 4

Me?

BETTY 3

As a Prologue.
You did so good.
I was right about you.

BETTY 4

Thanks. Thank you.

A moment between them. BETTY 3 takes her arm. On their way out the door:

BETTY 3

Bye Lion, thanks for the lovely dress-party-dinner-rehearsal.

BETTY 4

Bye Lion!

They're gone. BETTY 2 is alone. Ice cream and inflatables and beautiful, colourful chaos everywhere. BETTY 2 feels great peace.

BETTY 2

Bye everyone.

19. THE LAST REHEARSAL WHICH IS OPENING NIGHT WHICH IS A CATASTROPHE BECAUSE NOBODY SHOWS UP EXCEPT BETTY 2'S PUSSY.

A moment.
And then BETTY 2 finishes the last of her transformation. Maybe she strips down to her underwear. Maybe she does something else. However she does it, she achieves the final step toward the simplest and least guarded version of herself.

She faces us with confidence. She might come very very close to us.

BETTY 2'S PUSSY

Hello!
Hi!
I'm Betty's pussy.
I thought there was a show tonight?
Did none of the Betties come to The Thea-Tah?
That's sad.
That's too bad.
That's so irresponsible.
Or maybe it's liberated.
It's hard to tell the difference.
Anyway.
I'm here!
I'm usually more of a sort of a
behind-the-scenes type
if you will
but
OK
outside the comfort zone!
Yeah!
Carpe diem!

 BETTY 2'S PUSSY finds a guitar.

Oh! What's this!
For me?
OK.
Well.
That makes me think about
this song I wrote last night

    JEN SILVERMAN

and
nobody has ever heard it before
except for you.

> BETTY 2'S PUSSY *plays her song.*

> *The light narrows into a spotlight as she sings. She is very very good.*

SONG BY BETTY 2'S PUSSY

This is what I know about the world
there is light
it hits at an angle
it generates more light
I am bewildered and amazed by all the light.

This is what I know about the world
there are roads
there are bicycles and horses
tennis shoes and Porsches
there are unicorns oh maybe there aren't
I am bewildered and amazed by transportation.

There is so much that I don't know
I feel like it's generally OK to not know things
some people lie and pretend that they know what you mean
'Oh, I know what you mean!'
they say…
they say…
I don't say that unless I mean it,
and that is how I manage the things I don't know.

This is what I know about the world
it's not safe
it's strange and it's lonely
and mean but it's only
cuz everybody's scared
but it's probably gonna be OK
but that's unclear
but maybe not
but I don't know, I'm just a pussy!!

BETTY 2'S PUSSY finishes her song.

A moment. She smiles at us. Completely relaxed and at ease.

Blackout.

End of play.

SCORE

SONG by BETTY
BOOP 2's PUSSY

7/18/2016